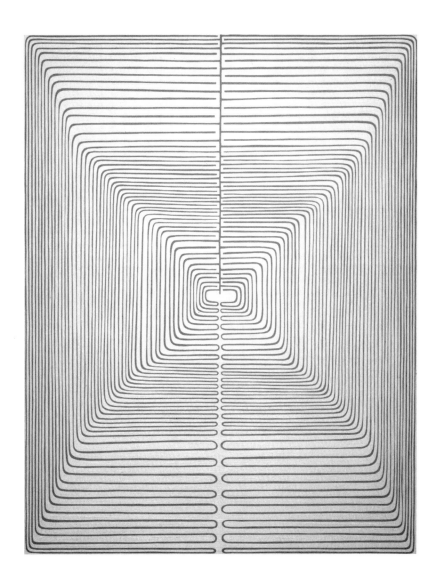

LIGHTS OUT

GEOFFREY YOUNG

For MP
+ JGP

lights
ON!

James S.

DRAWINGS
JAMES SIENA

THE FIGURES 2003

Cover painting: detail of "Eight Line Way," (second version), 19 x 15"
2001-02, by James Siena, courtesy of Daniel Weinberg Gallery.

Photograph of Billy Higgins, *Village Voice*, 1999

Acknowledgements to the editors of the following publications, where-
some of these poems first appeared: *Crayon, Mike & Dale's Younger Poets,
The Village Voice, Sulfur, New American Writing, Talisman, Poetry Archives
Newsletter-UCSD, Shiny, Shuffle Boil, The Hat, Poetry Project Newsletter, Stifled
Yawn, Berkshire Moments, The Best American Poetry 1988, Accomplices: Poems
for Stephen Rodefer* (Equipage, 2001), *The Blind See Only This World : Poems
for John Wieners* (Pressed Wafer/Granary, 2000), and in the chapbooks,
Elegies (Washington Project for the Arts, 1985), *Pockets of Wheat* (The
Figures, 1996 & 1998), *After the Fact* (Detour, 1998, thanks to Gary
Sullivan), *The Dump* (Cease Upon the Midnight, 2001), *Skate for Lunch*
(Cease Upon the Midnight, 2001) & *Space Jam by Billy Higgins* (Weary,
Stale, Flat & Unprofitable, Inc., 1999 & 2002).

With special thanks to Sharon & Trey Gregory, Katia Santibanez & Joe
Siena, Clovis & Ayler Young, Michael Gizzi for close reading, Sara Seagull &
Kenny Goldsmith for design skilz, and A. G. Rosen of the ever benevolent
Saul Rosen Foundation, without whose friendship and support this book
would not exist.

The Figures, 5 Castle Hill Avenue, Great Barrington, MA 01230
Distributed by SPD, 1341 7th Street, Berkeley, CA 94710-1403
Copyright © 2003 by Geoffrey Young
Drawings © 2003 by James Siena
ISBN 1-930589-19-0

CONTENTS

Et toi, beauté

Thrifty, Brave & Clean

The Dump

Ad-lib

Mount Trove Curry

Savoy

Space Jam by Billy Higgins

Lights Out

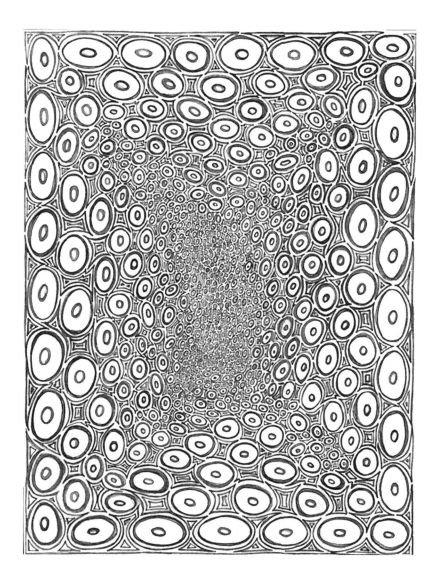

Et toi, beauté

I go over to my Sugar's shack
whenever I need a reminder
that "francophilia" is indeed
one of the five perversities.

HALO

If you don't
expect much

you won't be
disappointed.

THERAPY

You uncover the traces of a crime
you committed yourself. Hunting
for one thing you find another,
everything you come across is to
the point. No longer using aesthetic

criteria when every thing is social.
Some molecules are born illegal.
Others become so. The long arms of
the cranes turn, grip, lift and deposit
the rubble of an unspeakable day.

GET YOUR MIND RIGHT, GET YOUR GRIND RIGHT

Forgive me, practice, for ignoring
you lately. Days have a way of
filling up with manuscripts, mail
and minutiae. Too often I pick up

the phone, quick to say yes, you're on.
Like a dream image not jotted down
I lose the breathless humor of your
perfectly human emptiness. I'd sign

these words "Lonnie Shunyata" if I
thought you'd think the name cute.
Entanglements require my attention
now, but I want to go on record

as saying that not a day goes by
I don't think of you sitting on your
fanny, belly relaxed, eyes half closed
your still mind hot as the sun.

NEVER

A thing of beauty
will never hold the phone

just as the hunger for poetry
will never go unfed

MEPHISTO

Get into
the new beverage:

the Torquemada
Colada.

WITH LOVE

Intimacy issues
forth from
unadulterated

trust, a doorway
into a mansion

in which lust

is seen as
just what can happen
with love

HOW I BECAME A POST-MODERN SUBJECT

I saw Blue Mitchell in a ball of light
playing "Filthy McNasty"
on Mercer Street at dawn.

I hired a Waste Management Consultant
to streamline my excess energy.
I dreamt my parents enjoyed a happy

adulthood. I built a kunsthalle upon
a city of quotation marks, stoned
for walking on bottled water.

TRUE & FALSE

Flies don't fly in the dark
So can't harm an arm
Mercy falls when love crawls
You can walk it off in the city

Still weird to see the rapist in therapist
Brains know loss from gain
You can refuse to take calls, or return them
Your guest is as good as mine

LITTLE NARRATIVE

I don't buy future shock.
I say shoo-fly to all techno dreams
Flicking molecule-thick panaceas at my bean.

I like trumpet notes that scatter house cats
And writers who lift LIT by the scruff
Of its strides. Here's my NO vote
On heart-shaped beds. Give us this day
And room service instead. We'd never corrupt
A word. We can barely spell. Though this beak

Break on today's epiphenomena, we must
Capture rapture's little narrative
While all her Vladimirs say "Speak, memory."

ONCE

I heard a note
a very big beautiful note
played by Eric Dolphy on bass clarinet
a note that seemed to vibrate out

in one thick wave
to the back wall of the known universe
before returning
as if bouncing off that wall

in a flash through the void
with an elastic surge
still shaking with rhythm's
point of departure

JOE ING

We are not going
                    to be smart.
There are sings.
There are socks
                    a round bed.
The scissors bind
the bed. The scissors
fly. We are restless
but avoid them.
There is a well.
It avoids us.
It reveals us.
Notice! there are scissors above
the bed, huge scissor heads.
We must cut our legs.
We cannot cut our tongues.

AFTERNOON RUIN

Days, weeks, months smooth as a blister
like one long drink tipped back from Cinderella's slipper
with a fat pillow slipped behind your back
to read Whitman again

until it happens, as in video twilight, the retinal
after-image of the Twin Towers blocks all
you can see of Walt's loafing absence, leaving scattered
hearts pulverized with hideous pain.

Still you read his leaves, jumping
in the song's narrative shorebreak,
watching a dog trot by with a groundhog in its mouth
and spiders fatten on the blood of flies.

But these buildings will never be entered again
nor the people lost within them ever kissed.
Eyes burn as curbside doctors wait for patients
whose bodies no longer exist. Walt's dream amiss.

WHAT IF

The desire for heaven
is the desire to sexualize

death, if the born-again
bliss of sex is the need

to escape judgment and
doubt, if the end

of time is the moment
you come, *etcetera*?

LATE SEPTEMBER, 2001

Despite this brave new world
I have invested heavily in Barry
Bonds, whose steady stream of
Home runs is paying big dividends

In amazement, as he waits for a pitch
He can drive all the way to the bank
In Cooperstown, cash on the barrel
Head of baseball's deadliest bat

18 APRIL 1998

If you asked me now
what my favorite Monk tune was
I'd say, "Ask Me Now."

If you asked me how it goes
I'd say check out James Carter's
Jurassic Classics

but for the definitive time
hear the master himself
take it up on *Solo Monk.*

In small group format
Thad Jones and Charlie Rouse
trip its descending fantastic

on Monk's *Five By Monk*
reissued in a Milestone twofer
as *Brilliance* (vinyl)

the highlight of this date
being every last sound
in each and every groove.

UMA CON SALSA

I watched myself take Uma Thurman
away from a woman who was hitting on her
had to lift her down from a pedestal
where she sat wearing a crinkled pink

blouse for a photo shoot, even brushed up
against a nipple as we took off down
an alley, stopping to kiss every ten
feet or so on our way to eat burritos.

7 XII 84

What cafe table in Rome
Offers the best view of early Fellini?
What vat of crushed grapes stains
The whitewalls of the Pope Mobile?

Landscapes owe their horizons
To common sense, painters owe their brush
With mortality a color.
I owe this letter to Clark in Rome.

Under a gold leaf ceiling in the Vatican map room
He is dreaming of Jeanne Moreau
In *Moderato Cantabile*. I take his words as frames
In flicks. Hear his poems fucking names.

THE MATTRESS

This mattress must be turned
            over to The Romantic Poets
who just entered The Bank of England
            to steal a bag of money.

Like rain puddles trembling with starlight
            on a clear night sky
they are saying to the teller:
            "Ours was the last great century,"

"We are the last great English poets,
            you owe us." Back at the cottage
Dorothy's violin rests on William's desk,
            a desk that yearns for his head to fill it

with poems before The Romantic Poets
            take the money and walk back to
their Lake District hideaway to stash their
            loot under the mattress.

LIKE A CLOUD

Toss the shirt, Little Lulu,
& drop them dungarees, too.
I got a big boy's excitement in my smile
Because we can almost taste the hot dogs and french fries

The cosmos is about to deal us from its lobster pot
Of chrome zeros. Our martyrology's aboil now,
We're one with the one we love, advancing slowly
Toward the finish line and siesta. May air fills

The curtains with a breeze as from any position
We pass from ignition to perdition, as gods
—At least our big warm comforter thinks so.
Like a cloud it covers our holy tangled limbs.

ESCRITOIRE

Lester Bowie Rick Danko Ed Dorn
Guys whose sounds I've heard
For 30 years, gone within months.
Remember what the job cost them.

Listen to the way
They scaffold their voices.
As present as present can be,
All hold first chairs in eternity.

THE PERFECTING OF A NOTE

While at one moment
she could not understand the ease
with which she felt a stranger to a past
that had once been as close to her as her own body

and at the next moment
she could not understand
how anything could ever have been
different from the way it was now, something

else occurred to her.
Now and then it happens that
one sees something in the distance,
an unfamiliar thing, and walks toward it

and at a certain point
that thing enters into the circle
of one's own life, but the place where
one was before is now strangely empty.

WHAT'S WITH GRAVITY

What I mean by gravity is charity
the self as found object
redefining "life size"

humor and horror depicted
in scenes on a dirtbike
of emotion, competing for awards

in metal, glass and timeless
paradox. And this: it begins
in secret, becomes sole desire,

is kept uneasy by hugeness
of need, then settles in like
second nature, only it's the first.

IN HER COURTNEY LOVE FASHION

Lauren was saying that sometimes,
when overweight, she faked

orgasms, like when Josh would be
thrusting away all she could hear was

the "thubble thubble thubble"
of the extra flesh on her thighs
wrecking whatever pleasure
she was supposed to be having.

RAY CHARLES

Which comes first: the art form
Or the social conditions that spawn it?

The world is divided into anecdotes and
Money. Money is divided into oil and hunger.

Oil is too slippery to mention in the desert
Of the poem. Ray is to me what I am to him:

Pure hospitality. Never
Exceeded, rarely equalled.

FINDING A MOREL

To tell everything
exactly as it happened

requires magnitudes
of self-control

in order to tell nothing
beyond what happened

WHEN I CONSIDER

The influence of Fats Waller's
            "Honeysuckle Rose"
on Charlie Parker's
            "Scrapple from the Apple"

I feel like an antiquated fad
            of the information age
but can you help me express
            how "Round Midnight"

relates to "Embraceable You"
            and "Naima" answers
"In a Sentimental Mood"?
            I'm not talking about

dropping the final "e" on
            subjectiv. Call
and response
            at its most attuned.

VENERY

And its adjective, "venereal," are most often thought of
    as signifying physical love
        From Venus the Latin root *ven*
which appears in the word *venari*, means "to hunt game"
    In *Origins*, Eric Partridge asserts that
        the ven in venari has its original meaning
"to desire, and therefore, to pursue"
    & he sees a close connection between it & the word "win"
        from the Middle English *winnen*,
and even the Sanskrit *vanoti*, "he conquers"
    It is in this sense that venery came
        to signify the hunt and it was so used in all the early
works on the chase, including the earliest known

on the subject of English hunting
Le Art (sic) *de Venery*
in Norman French in the 1320's

for Lyn Hejinian

FRANK

O'Hara made friends poems and the world
is a thing called Joe, the city owes him a lane
of walls matter with gorgeous tragedies
but no two artists swing the same. Like happiness
hanging on them. If we stand still and shut up
The strike zone is a variable foot and a half wide,
pictures hit us in a space they create
He knew where the dipsos went to bibulize.
for themselves, somewhere between image
black bags and curiosity kills the crap.
collapse and surface sizzle. Here, affection
pays attention as sidewalks disappear under

FOURTH WALL

Say one thing, mean another
You're a writer, writing.
On the open side of the stage
People think they can see you.

Society's entirely spoken
By stream-lined incredible
Women. Sugar on the pill
Of logic can be swallowed later.

Look alive. All god's buttons front
The same tender genderwear.
We're dressed to thrill, we're very
Prêt à party. "Au reservoir, dawg."

FOR TONY TOWLE

In my case, adaptation means
new wheel bearings and new tires
if I am ever to leave the garage
in which Tony maps his main
inspirations. Blue is not a color

we can normally afford to live
without. Time reaches back
farther than our genes seem
to go. Guests make cleaning
the house an acceptable necessity.

I'm dusting this room to make
space for Tony's new & selected.
It is easier to build a shrine
when there are unemployed
gods ready to inhabit it.

INSECT ASIDE

Hitting the gallery streets every few buildings run into
someone we know, encounters resembling to a remarkable
degree the collisions of ants in the throes of work.
Hustling up and down stairs, conversation is conducted

through antennae manipulated frenetically by the rumor
of prices, by the news of some "devastating upheaval" or
"redemptive folly" which vitally concerns the entire anthill.
In the morning fatigue, images, tea, scraps of paper, calls.

AUTOBIOGRAPHY

Puts the past in handcuffs
And marches it down Main Street

The way taffy stretched in the present
Snaps. Like a fighting fish in a real-time dive

Autobiography's hooked on what's my line.
The right details make fabulists of us all.
Toward what end then? Live the bit again?
"Ink spills." So the story goes.

OH MODERN MUSE

of powerlessness, who shields me
from the over-familiar treasure
of rhyme, and condemns me to condense
as I reread, please wrap me in your
implacable vocabulary, make me one

with those inaccessible masters whose
example we champion, saved from
perfidious drunkenness and undue
melancholy by direct perception
of the world, dedicating like a guage

of love these few lines of my life
written on the backs of envelopes
and receipts while driving a zippy
imported sedan, or seated in the dark
at dawn inspired by the folds in your

drapery and your curled locks, help me
to forge (what is the word) the poem's
pure passion, which today bears
the shape of woman or man, but
tomorrow may well be a house pet.

TIME OUT

A blue jay the size of a blue jay
standing in a stream of snow melt
flowing down a rut in the access road
behind the house
for two brief seconds
dips his beak in the water and chug-a-lugs!

the sun shining on his omniattentive
eyes, until something, or just
the fear of something,
spooks him, and with one quick hop
he disappears into the low
branches of a row of hemlocks.

FRESH IMPRESSIONISM

With his famous buck slash stutter-step
Walter Payton was *le chef d'école*
of motion, line and hard-hitting color
making his mark stand up against

the best opposing forces of Sunday afternoon
avant-pigskin smashmouth
shade and power anywhere
no matter what century, *en plein aire*

POEM TO THE YOUNG

To see what condition my condition is in
I've had a drink and it's making me think of
John Singer Sargent's great "Robert Louis Stevenson"
seated in a wicker chair, and of urging you
to read ten-thousand books, including *Footsteps*

by Richard Holmes, while you're still
free to wander, free to hope, and free to love.

IMPROVISATORI

This has everything to do
          with boiling the water
that goes into saying what
          this moment's otherwise
imprecise and mysterious
          big IT is all about, while
sipping from a cup made
          hot with tea given this
poem by April Gornick.

THE HAPPIEST MAN ALIVE

Utter turmoil, anger, disbelief
the candid admission that we are only
so capable, *so* inclined, that we fall silent
mid-sentence, disconnected inside

that our own conflicts bore us
that fears of old age and failure are
as embarrassing as cheap despair is
ludicrous, calling even "Nothing" into question

haunted, dread-seized, floating along on heavy
wings but low on fuel, as darkness falls
looking for the lights of a landing strip
looking for a town without self-pity

THIS YEAR'S EMILIA BASSANO AWARD

for Dark Lady of Off Broadway
goes to you, sweetheart, in lieu of a Tony.
Who else so richly deserves
to be honored for seduction,
manipulation, and ever ambiguous charm?
What other muse has so capably

conjured the double-time, the maybe baby,
the "I never said I loved you" line
making this fan a fool and you a snare
that others following in my footsteps
will try their innocent luck at. Now I can
honor you for what you've done, and won.

HAIR CROWNS

When East meets West fashion spills
over the body in a continuous round of fittings
while eyes, once again outlined in red, develop

highlights that flatter the summer tan designed
with today's sporty women in mind. Small
patterns, preferably white on black, allegorize

a T-shirt for a mule. Today's catwalk is imported
coral beach sand shot behind the scenes with
surrealist accessories. Teased by a machine

wind, hair crowns the impact of new forms.
Tall forms, thin forms. So tall, so thin, so
very tall and thin.

SANDWICH

She walks in beauty to the refrigerator
thinking "Goodbye columbine of August,
goodbye glassy lake, yellowjackets, trowel,

mildewed towels," adding, "farewell complete
thoughts of a genius written on a half sheet
of notepaper." Sensing the list growing

rudderless, she docks there, just as a ruler
measures itself, to remember that Kipling
wrote *The Jungle Book* while living in Vermont.

NAME

At night I think about it
by day I have no idea where it went
walk from room to room
pick up envelope, manuscript,
telephone, call C, M, A

evening tired on the sofa
a plate of food & glass of water
my ear still listening
the web that is the past
asks what happened, I am

feeling for the spot, when I
sip it it's wet the food goes
down vegetable I never know
what it's going to say
till I read it later

WHEN I SEE A TRAIN
I WANT TO TAKE IT IN MY ARMS

Observation
raised to the level of all-embracing consciousness
weaves a bird's nest in Whitman's beard
below mountains turning brown, grey,
      before disappearing under snow until Spring.

The person formally known as O'Shea Jackson
raps in a home-made
patchwork quilt toga.
A yoga teacher prunes a tree.
      Wind "dithers" in a valley of aspen.

We're waist-deep in the alpenglow,
rotating Bill Evans, Ahmad,
Elmo and Herbie Nichols on the box.
For all these, as you please,
      add figs for Aristophanes.

GEOFFREY YOUNG

I am light, comfortable,
and best of all, I really work.
I'm still headquartered here

but production takes place
nearly anywhere, having come
a long way from the scissors,

tape, and drawing board
of just a decade ago
on the coast. The inspiration

remains the same, however.
To create works that provide
style, insight, and durability

for active people of all ages.
Thank you for choosing
"Geoffrey Young."

Thrifty, Brave & Clean

"The place, I'll make it all the same, I'll make it in my head, I'll draw it out of my memory, I'll gather it all about me, I'll make myself a head, I'll make myself a memory, I have only to listen, the voice will tell me everything, tell it to me again, everything I need, in dribs and drabs, breathless, it's like a confession, a last confession, you think it's finished, then it starts off again"

Samuel Beckett *The Unnamable*

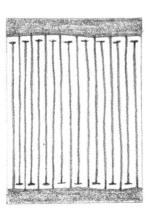

DRIVE, IT SAID

I was in love with a song, kept blurting it out, didn't know the words, maybe something about gazing at stars, I do that too, the constellations like old friends, but I might have been in a hot desert wearing snowshoes, the song would not let me go, I was like someone in love, that was the name of the tune in fact, I played it on the trumpet for the ghost of Kenny Dorham, even missing the highest note out of respect for Kenny's "flat on his ass" style, this song was leading me to something, wasn't it? There was no love in my life, or there *was* love, children are loves, brothers and sisters and old friends are love, even the dog is love, but when the fire in the hearth goes out there's no love, no love served at the table, time to get up, time to leave. My candor is true even if my art is grave. Certainly there was no feeling of new love, no baptismal life-blood romance excitation stirring up the emotions, the months plodding by, celibate eternities curiously bearable. Like an experiment in sensory deprivation these months would go on the soul's résumé, though I didn't feel noble, strong, or medieval. Rather sad and exhausted. It's hard to swallow a family, tough to cling to what is no longer there. I could ask for a show of hands here, yes, I could ask for a show of hands.

Hollow at the center of the chest, my lungs, and underneath a shirt my heart hurt. It was a constant pain, it wasn't painful, it was ponderous. I felt closer to everybody on the street, to the people I didn't know, the disfigured and halt, the guy with the huge goiter on his neck standing with his little dog on the storefront sidewalk. I felt tender toward the scruffy kids in the neighborhood whose fathers were in jail or drunk, people who'd gone through it, or were about to, it hurt to see them, one big unhappy family starring everyone. I was poised on that point where measurement fails, the body clamped in on itself, bruised, the little light pleasures of taste and sound were difficult to endure, hard to put two or three thoughts together, reason through an essay, move from sofa to chair, and back, finally standing up to wolf down a sandwich—single people always eat standing up at the sink—just as love compels me to this dialect, says "take a walk, drive around neighborhood, look at houses, read their stiff faces, their colors, their porches, count glass in windows divided into panes, smell smoke from chimneys, see formal snowshovels." So much was up in the air, so many moments I'd turn to a last falling leaf, or a dashing cat, and want to speak, say "What's up?" or "Where are the boys?" Elements of an unraveling tale written by squirrels in the circular sockets of a brain, I was eager for duties, for the demands of a job, contact with real people around a real table. I am literal, lived-in, to think out loud is not to say much until it's written. Give me a life in turmoil so I can feel what size brushstrokes will convey its portrait, the set of jaw, eyes the way the painter saw them, slipping. Home-made tapes accompanied my long commutes, driving *was* music, music never sounded more fundamental, like a dictionary come alive, it entered bodily, it was purposeful direction, all touch and go. I didn't know any teenage girls flipping out, didn't have to include that sound. Sometimes silence and the humming car would take on the shape of domestic anger's impossible heavy life sentence, no one to blame, not even myself, or the culture, a vicious spear thrust into the shell of the alien other, it hit me, I closed up around it, a sea anemone. Why do we hold on to the pain, perform heroic measures to sustain an embalmed identity? Why not melt into it and notice a seagull's beak.

Or I would begin to flirt with desire for the very change I feared, to be free of the rasps, to be on my own again, be my own boss, make my own clichés, hang my own pictures, dial my own information, less security, but more adventure, less friction, more desire, click the lights off, knock back the heat and slip upstairs to read late into the night, a light that disturbs no one, a few pillows behind the back, a notebook on the nightstand, you can see me here, I'm covered from head to toe, it's an 18th Century classic, it's a copy of *Tears On My Pillow*, it's the neo-wave of the present, I'm wide awake, there's so much to read, so many sentences to speak out loud, words to prowl.

The bedside clock ticks, it's a different tune, it sings, "Take care of yourself and get plenty of rest," then sleep like a sponge drops, sops up awareness, involuntary muscular jerks unkink the self, a distant voice whispers "Take the night off, Lonesome. You can't just have these emotions, you gotta pay for 'em." I was like someone in love falling asleep alone, but only *like*, there was no one there but memory, but fear. Cold mornings the sun would tip through the east facing windows and arrive on my skin all but extinguished, the light bouncing off the snow a multi-vitamin. And curious people would tour the little house, it was amusing, I didn't own it, things began to fill it, tables on loan, sofa too, I'd be self-conscious, apologize for the bow in the shelves containing the poetry books, made 'em myself, the rooms so small my eyes could travel the spines, I could jump out of bed and reach the volume of my choice and be back under the covers before the mattress knew I'd left. Sometimes I think everything I know I've learned from poems, then I wake up, I see whole rooms exactly as they were, filled with paintings, I think I'm still in them, the Malevich room at the Stedelyk in Amsterdam, it's a space-station on the trajectory of abstract art, I sit back down and watch it orbit, it's supreme.

My dreams these mornings weren't spectacular, some revenge, some lust, but the big gnawing fact relentless and obsessive was there to greet me at dawn, a broken record, a tapeloop, in the video version the fact planted its green flag in my face, I was its imagery's victim, even as the credits went rolling by, our distant vows went back into the can for the next night's showing, beginning middle and end, finito, history, join the club. I bought a TV set and played the remote buttons like a thumb piano, it broke the silence, it lit the walls, and at dusk I'd say to myself, as I reached for the lamp, "Light the first light of evening," in stentorian tones, or "His gorgeous self-pity." So much for darkness then, but the darkness was only more apparent in the lamplight, I couldn't see where I was going, the body, my own, the room like a cage, moving from chair to sofa, legs tucked up under for warmth, a blanket, a magazine, I was 85 years old, I was fifteen, a manuscript was my afghan, a pile of mail, then the hop-up adrenalin of a phone call, let's have another show of hands here, you've been there too, it's ringing just for you, the miniscule bag of groceries, silent rice, passing moments passing, sponged whiteness of stove, sink, all the books filed away, the rug unwalked on, records in alphabetical order, a new ribbon, a stack of envelopes, the liquid paper crust that fell as white dots swept into the trash, I was puttering, not paralyzed, I was waiting, I remembered hitch-hiking through Bulgaria with a Lebanese guy in a two door sedan, and stopping to share cigarettes in a village off the main road. People suddenly materialized, we were surrounded, they looked at our clothes, we exchanged furtive smiles, kidded with the children, then out of nowhere a woman advances, hands us a just baked loaf of bread, it's big and round and solid and warm and we are immediately touched, we thank them, I shake the woman's hand, it is callused and rough, her eyes are light brown, they are filled with amber lines that seem to spin, while my hands are soft, I'm bookish, I'll sleep tonight on the floor of the train station in Sofia, use my bookbag for a pillow, be up early fully dressed still and away. Is there still a crust of that bread?

Later, picked up in Yugoslavia by a Persian driving a truckload of rugs to Munich, you want to hear about this guy? I believe my senses, I finally had to escape from him in Vienna, completely unstrung me, he was single-minded devotion, we shared five words in English, and one night at a truckstop outside Zagreb, about midnight of a moonless starry night, we stopped to eat, he propositioned our blond waitress, we finished the meal, and she followed us out to the truck, got in between us, we drove a mile down the road, pitchblack. He pulled to the side and stopped. He grabbed a blanket from the cab, they got out, they disappeared into the featureless landscape. Is this the freebooting life of adventure so ably described in *Tropic of Cancer*? Could one say "No," in Serbo-Croatian? Is there a God? I can't see them out there. Then just as suddenly as the truck had stopped, and they'd gotten out, she was back, alone, she was furious, she grabbed her jacket from the cab, she was livid, her light summer dress fit her perfectly, she slammed the cab door and took off walking down the highway, back to her truckstop. What had my Persian rug man done to earn her disapproval? He got back to the truck, threw the blanket in the cab, shrugged his shoulders, and off we drove into the night, there were borders to cross, spring flood waters rushing off the Alps to admire. By the time we got to Vienna, after some harrowing driving routines in dense traffic, some lane-changing leaps of faith that only a true son of Allah's compassionate protection could have gotten away with, he finally pulled off into a side street, it was about eight in the evening, we stopped, he looked over with a smile and said "Girls" (that was one of the five words we shared), and smiled, reached under the front seat, brought out a razor, a mug with soap, a brush, some cold water from a bottle, and a filthy hand towel, and proceeded to lather the soap for his evening shave, daubing cold water on his bristly dark beard, and glancing over at me as if to indicate, What An Evening We'll Have! But listening to him pull that dull razor across his cold scraped cheeks I nearly gagged, he was really hacking, nicking chin and cheek, his blood-stained towel on the seat I wouldn't touch with a shoe. I had to cut, jam, no time to get sick, I thanked him for the lift, he looked surprised, I was abandoning him!

Where was my sense of fun? I grabbed my bag, opened the cab door, swung down, waved once, and took off walking down the city street. It was meant to be, back on my own two feet, and all aboard for the night train to Munich, I was on it, now it's the next day, it's two in the afternoon and I've just eaten a bratwurst and drunk a beer, I turn a corner and nearly bump into the only person I know in all of Germany, a girlfriend named Brigitte Gapp with a Marilyn Monroe-like birthmark on a pale cheek, dark hair, big bright smile, I go crazy, this is serendipity writ large, Jung's magic synchronicity, we fall into each other's arms, we stare, the only person I know, how account for it? The mind entertains a wisdom that the body can't understand.

People would say it takes a year, maybe two, there was money on the table, there were things, what was spoiled needed division, a few rounds of letterhead legality meetings on creamy stationery, the feints and dodges, the disclosures, the aggressive silence, the screaming meemies, the three-piece options expert, the comma that allows, insists, *demands* another term, something must follow the end of the world, this one here, the oil burner clicks on, these words cost money, it was happening to other people too, it was commonplace, you could join a group and discuss it, commiserating phone calls from old friends long since lost track of, the word spreads, a postcard from a woman in New York wanting to meet, we've mutual friends, let's have a drink together, a movie-nut uptown, I'd really like her, the chorus chorused, she's just breaking up with, this is the network speaking, it's an erotic universe of random strangers coupling, the matchmakers were lighting up, they closed their cover before striking, life could resume, don't hesitate, change your sheets, act like someone in love would act, get that bounce back into your step, kid, talk funny again, and all so nice and young. *Quel* sequence. It's typical though, isn't it? There's more variety in a crisis, more sense of drama in the pain of a social hello. To be on the crest of a breaking wave, but would you get smashed to the sand and ground up, or ride it for all it's worth into a new life, stolen like fire from the gods one burning finger at a time? Drive, it said, digitalized, accessed, therapied, the talk in every cafe on Main Street. This is our human universe, the glue on a chipped cup, this end that signals a new beginning is the cheapest gas in town. I drink it myself.

1987

SERUM BERNHARD

We meet someone at the right moment
we take everything we need from them
we give them everything we have, and then
we leave them, again at the right moment.

We adapt ourselves to the mentality and
temperament of a person, and for a time
we take in only what this person's mentality
and temperament have to offer us, and when

we think we've taken in enough, when we've
had enough, when we've given all we have to give,
we simply sever the connection. We spend
years sucking all we can out of someone,

and then, having almost sucked them dry,
we suddenly say that we ourselves are being
sucked dry, we simply see that we ourselves
are being sucked dry. And for the rest of

our lives we have to live with the knowledge
of our own baseness. Because there are
some people you must escape from
rather than let yourself be devoured.

BURGER KIM

Been dumped, been resurrected, heard a Quaker
whaler hymn "all hands on Dick," yet still I plump it,
grasp at cathedral stone, grip the moon's blind
backside like a flea on bended knee, my Tutsi
scrolls good for nothing but rolling your Hutu credits.

Because you know what it's like to exit a photo booth
into the fatty tissue of daylight, please drape your
shades on the knob and slip into something invisible,
Mistinguette, while I sprint my sneaks home from the
gym. I only want to hire your finger for ring storage.

But then, parched lawns, barking trees, no go, zut!
My search engine falls to the sand a coconut
thrashed in a gale. If you could just take my head
in stride, Carmelina, watch me go all ceiling spackle
boron flaky with skinhead tonsure, we could call this

tune by its rightful nomenclature. Our grill's in
earnest, we know from Chilean seabass, as we know
why John Donne ain't here to re-write. But yes,
Little Egypt, you must cut "Wild Thing" on my
Pregnant Bank label. Let ottava rima throw a hissy fit.

"Here" creates "there," and "there" trashcans the
stupendisoid. I should hate "Hey, Joe," but it taught
me the long way to swift monosyllables. What's in
the sack? Your ball toss? I'm hardly breathing,
I'm over-prepared for sleep. As bamboo was the thing

to panda Hsing-Hsing, I'm following your
breadcrumb trail through a food court, asking
"Is this picture worth a thousand cokes?"
I'm in bad need of an exorcism, Deirdre.
No Canyon of Heroes will receive our motorcade

though I still love your range in the hole, and all
that go-go in slo-mo emotion. The sum is dim
and your gingko drives me nuts. I crack a toothy.
Have you ever plastered an afternoon's hamstring?
I miss the bliss and bale of your roundhouse right.

An ancient Greek rowing song inspires us
to pull our way to the mountain top, Ginger,
for it was I who took the first steps toward you,
and it will be I crawling through your garden
after hours. Let me explain why it is dusk, dry,

damaging. Because the arugula makes me do it.
Here's a cowbell, Evangeline. Say something.
Crunch your soft abs for extra fruition,
for seigneurial swagger, for the right to flash
that red smile. I know the way your heel fits

in my hand is very "tragic foot," but great pasta
requires great sauces. Coping skills merely
polish us off. Let's sneak a peek under the hood,
add a pinch of salt to this Great Barrington hunch.
It just might catch your falling star for lunch.

WRITING IS AN AID TO MEMORY (16 April 1997)

Wake Thursday morning on John & Karen's sofa under
Wilsey's cat, a slight head from last night's vino, hear
John's footsteps creak down stairs and remember it's
Clovis' 23rd birthday, his 23rd spring, feel pangs of Clovee
pride in stride with bright forsythia & blooming daffodils.
Lie there plotting the day's walk to Wall Street for lunch with
Zaharo (a walk in which I succumb to CD temptation at J & R,
buying four). She'd flown to KC the day before, got home late,
was tired, but we eat and talk, and she says, "I'd invite you
to spend the night on my sofabed if I weren't dead." "But I want
to sleep with you," I say (first uncautious words of this kind),
and she doesn't miss a beat, "That's what they all say."
Then race uptown on the 4 train to 59th and Lex to POLO

at 650 Madison (dark wood, plaid pillows, horse prints)
for a meeting with Ralph's 22 year old daughter Dylan
and his VP of Art Direction, Carter, a-flag-logo-on-white-
sweater-wearing wonderwoman, assigned, it seems, the task
of helping to shape young Dylan's business urges, as am I,
somehow, become a consultant-fantasist, thanks to Karen Grant's
suggestion, steering the girl's dreams of a glorified youth scene
with bar, gallery, good lighting, performance space, daytime
coffee, and microwaveable food, even though it's not clear
she's ever worked a day in her life. As the meeting ends I
caution her to get a job at a cafe, bar, gallery or restaurant
in order to know what workers actually experience, then cab
a quick fifteen blocks to the Whitney to meet AG in its new

library quarters, leaving a note for the absent librarian May
Castleberry, before going upstairs to view a Vija Celmins
drawing hanging in the Biennial that Renee McKee—after we
pestered her for a year to get one—is offering AG a crack at,

and with great anticipation (drum roll crescendo), we turn
the corner and see it (crashing cymbals of hail bop!), and it is
beautiful, a night sky with distant trace of comet, wondrously
quiet & fastidiously sustained, so off we go like two fireflies
in a bonfire down 5th Avenue to McKee to tell Renee it's a go,
& to pay her for a Jeanne Silverthorne piece bought in December.
We both wish we didn't feel burnt from last night's splashy
Drawing Center Benefit because we could imagine celebrating
the Celmins score with a bottle of champagne, but instead

proceed to Robert Miller to preview the Julio Galan show
opening later in the evening, where Massimo Audiello takes us
through the annex to see Robert Polidori's photos of *salles*
in the palace of Versailles undergoing renovation, leading us
into the back room to see smaller Polidori works as well
as a group of Gursky photos we'd never seen, buying nothing but
two Galan catalogues. Another cab takes us back up Mad. to 75th
to get AG's Rover, pointing its gas-starved hood ornament over
to 10th Avenue in the 30s to buy $40 worth. Then we pull in
front of Matthew Marks on 24th so I can run in and see Inez's
photos, and Nayland Blake's installation of bunny drawings,
but the most surprising thing I see in a small side gallery
is a mid-size drawing by Terry Winters (he's now with Marks)

of pinkish-red thatched lines, in oil pastel. Next door Metro
shows me Tip's so-called "Jerry Speyer" painting,
and for a change I don't know, so off we drive around
a few corners to Cheim & Read's to view Juan Uslé's new work
(photos very like his paintings, and a few paintings, including
a great little one AG says Ron Low has on reserve). Around
a few more blocks (we take turns going in to see the shows)
we check out the two Uslé's Carol Greene is selling and AG picks
the better of the two, and now, with time running out, and
because we're shot, AG steers the ride down Varick toward my car,
dropping me near the entrance to the Holland Tunnel into which

he will descend on his way to join Debi for dinner in New Jersey, everyone looking forward to a good night's sleep. But not before

I buy salad bar food in a deli to eat in the car as I drive up the Westside Highway sipping a Peach Snapple, getting almost to the Peekskill exit listening to a radio broadcast of the Yankees-Brewers game (David Cone doesn't have his good stuff), when, overcome with fatigue, I pull off the Taconic and drop into an hour long coma. When I wake, the Yankees are up 4-2 on a Tino Martinez HR, but soon it is 4-4, and then crackle crackle, transmission begins to fail. Now home, I wonder who won the game, thinking back to yesterday's encounters in Soho while viewing shows by Walton Ford (birds), Fred Tomaselli (birds), and Jane Hammond (the state of Connecticut), before I walked down West Broadway to the Soho Grand Hotel to meet for the first time the young Duke graduate Dylan Lauren.

THE COVER LETTER

Enclosed please find
my distinctively postmodern
bourgeois notions, within which

I trace the negative dialectic
to its resting place (herein radicalized)
in domestic phenomenology,

positing itself at the center of identity,
exclusionary and logocentric
effects which defy narrativity

even as they elaborate systems
of domination from beginning to end
in a rather bizarre defiance

of reading itself. Interventions
impose their ambiguities,
to truncate irony, to pique your

interest. I could get you going,
a paean to Adorno's adage, or just
the opposite truth. Fragmentation thus

is coherence, like the pitch of a flat
roof, yielding to genius and pluck. I beg
you to consider my length.

MORNING OF THE WIDE FLOORBOARDS

"He loved pepper and zigzag lines."
Lichtenberg

"You can't sit too close to a piano," the Raj said,
"Or harbor seals in a dried up lakebed. Mirages
Crack with a hissing sound. Don't ask me why.
You can hear better with an ear of corn."

Then the genius pounced his rag paper,
Uncapped his pen, and watched objects fly up
Into the air of his brain and hang there
Like renaissance angels above a mattress.

Was he sketching, or kvetching? The Raj
Was given to the motto, "Each mile, each
Hermaphrodite," offered like hors d'oeuvres
To his second banana. "This is my delicious

Little machine for pulverizing ancestors," he crowed.
The Raj was known for always having the right
Tote bag for the occasion, and by now, even the
People who still smoked knew it was the Raj

Himself who'd installed the Marlboro Man
In Madame Tussaud's Wax Museum. Buried on page
Six, yes, but it was news nevertheless.
The country as a whole had watched Virginia

Go down hill, trebly tired of offering her weak
Defense on the sensuality of smoke. Her passport-
To-visability mask clung to her wrinkles
Like a shoehorn. Suddenly, the spin cycle whistled

To a clunky halt. The Raj's poodle was lifted
Into a basket, taken outside, and hung up. It was

Hat Day, and the extensive yellow tape demarcating
The crime scene only permitted passage to the police.

The atmosphere braced itself against sunstroke.
The Raj was struck by the sky's almost touchable blue.
"There are only two kinds of adventurers," he
Proposed, "Those who lead by leaving, and those

Who lead by laughing." The Raj surveyed the wondrous
Zeitgeist, which included Tom, crouching
In the shade, waiting for Jerry to land nearby.
Poetry drinks water from a sealed bottle.

Then the decade approached, a libertine with a wallet.
But the Raj faced the ocean spray with his cool gaze
Set on any eventuality, ready to represent. "We will
Drive through the park unharmed," he elucidated.

Though clearly too late to die young, it was perhaps
Still too early for him to live it up. The Raj was not
For the moment. He was for eating Chinese, later.
There were just a few good hours of sunlight left.

SPLASHED WITH EAU DE PHILOSOPHER KING

They say it's 30,000 light years
    to the center of the word
for the finger that points to bright blankness.
    Come on, Buddha! I prefer the guy
who trapped a positron
    for two months and named it Priscilla.
If properly understood
    it is possible to troop forth "replenished"
by the roundabout fact of a detour
    but what approaches now is
the steam cleaning hour
    the mauve trickle suck-egg
dénouement crushed hopes
    wracked with guilt
love your children's eyelashes hour,
    c'est à dire, the "I don't want
to have to go around anything" moment
    least of all right now
when leaves curl forth on April stems and pollen
    readies itself for a fall.
We're here, we're self-destructive
    we've got nothing but ourselves to fear
though what's neurotic is still exotic
    and right before our eyes
if only a tiny fragment of it will survive.

OUT OF THIS WORLD—Fall 1965

"Hey Carl, these mikes are doing us wrong."
J. C.

The deepest recesses of subjectivity blown up
We were driving from Santa Barbara to L.A.
To hear Coltrane live it was our first chance
Worried we wouldn't get a seat
At the It Club on Washington Boulevard

Mobbed, we thought, every kid with a record player
Will be lined up to hear the man
Who stands for all that we aspire to
With his crux sound precision tendril stamina mind
As we passed the waves at Rincon

Thinking back to the day a month earlier when
We got run off some gorgeous three foot rights
By Jesus! it's Marshall Dillon of *Gunsmoke*
Legendary square-jawed redheaded James Arness riding a huge
Old surfboard, "OK, Jim, you're the law, we'll accommodate you"

Prick!   Then we're chugging up, we're over, we're
Coasting through the San Fernando Valley, closing in
Will Elvin be there? Will Bo's fake i.d. pass
Stopping for gas and another quart of oil
Dropping off a hitch-hiker who thanks us with

The then common regional signoff, "Much grass"
We're hoping he'll play "Impressions" and "Naima"
And the immortal long intro solo on "I Want To Talk About You"
If we can get in, if we don't have to
Listen from the sidewalk outside

We're slowing down for the offramp
A few more unfamiliar blocks and

Let's lose this oil-belching heap! Cheap enough
Door, but we only have enough money
For three of the four of us to get in

Which leaves Roger the Lodger, with no i.d., no
Wallet—he didn't even bring shoes!—out
So Roger just walks away with a smile
As Paul and Bo and I enter the It
And the It's almost empty! A few tables filled, glasses

Half-drained, but no college kids from SC or UCLA
Was I wrong to think so? We're the only white guys
In the place, and there are precious few blacks
To hear *the* tenor of our time, the horn
With the form to fire the brain and carve

Huge caverns of feeling in the chest
With his lush lyric mathematics
Mais où sont les oreilles? Was Malcolm X shot today?
No. World Series game on TV? Ditto.
It's dark, smokey, a blues on the juke

As we sit like pashas in a red leather booth
Directly in front of where the bell
Of his horn will be, not two yards away
And so close to McCoy's bench we will graph
His digit audacities in dart space

Thus sipping tiny nodes of social outrage
And secret glee we wait like sphinxes
For the members of the band to emerge and ask
Their question, which they finally do, silently, without
Fanfare, downbeat fall on us! when with an unobtrusive lift

Of the horn the quartet begins to fill the air
With intricate singing figures and cascade chords

Stretched tune to tune, reservoirs of emotion
Probed more deeply than we'd ever gone
They were so endless, tunnelling into ear and heart

Like to transform our bodies, realign our souls
Making life's absurdities meaningful by reinventing beauty
With pulses articulated from Love's
Perfect pain, perfect annihilation, perfectly registered
Lines to light our speechless body's glowing night

WRITTEN BEFORE A BRICE MARDEN PAINTING
WHILE WAITING FOR LEAH OLLMAN AT MATTHEW MARKS
ON MADISON AVENUE, APRIL 21, 1993

Tangle my eye in these no age webs
Of ghost gray, dusk blue lines or lime.
This scratched and wandering head's unbowed,
Lit by erasures, lit by the way time

Loops up, reaches over, falls like
Hair. In this circuitry, curved space
Cooly stares, shaggy supple washes go any
Where, like pearls hanging from gears.

Let's nibble trail mix on dale hikes
To a stretch of squat toad color
Before a scour notches a shortcut
With shingles that wing, directioning.

What ointment? A pilgrimage? We cross
Roads coarse with crabshells to look beyond
Scent. Let his ambling body's modesty
Return upon itself to what's meant.

As in he means to sustain, he
Means to send scribblers a pile
Of straight twigs that snap, setting bones
Plain as juncture, open, as laps.

HIS UNEXAMPLED SAMPLES

What I am wants
                    but waits
        impatiently
and so we reach
        the year 1907
introducing these few
        incidentals:
    to *muse*
                    derives from
the medieval Latin
        for snout, to sniff
      around, to cast about
for a scent
        looking down
                    and out
        from a room
in which Whalen's
            fabled lens enlarges

but wants now, here, spring
        sun on stunned
      tulips, too cold to grow
today's this desktop
        quick jot
not enough
      that it's hot enough
                on Venus
        to melt lead
if we're to understand
        extinction
contemplate Nemesis
        turn up the flame

break in half
        for a name

wants me now as its own
a promontory so sacred
        there were little
piles of money on it
        that no one
            would touch,
            foyer of a huge
vocabulary mint, ever
        the attentive stint in
progress, Succuba as
        cheeping bird, as word
        received from
                    a totally dis-
interested power

March 22, 1989 for Clark Cooldige

ELEGY LY III

Clouds of fingerlings roiling in a blue tank
and for movement here comes the man with the bucket.
Watch 'em hit! especially early in the present tense.
We'll be investigating the evidence of a less
coordinated raid before their snapping jaws close.
Perspective is what changes the pursuit. Just by
giving up a little we become effective bright-mouthed
coastal omnivores, implanting something, shall we say,
pure in the mirror? We've all seen it. The face,
the big face, some god-awful big face belonging
to no one, round as a nickel. Our father's?

He is sad. You can't ask. He cries watching
"The Gambler, The Nun and The Radio" on TV. He
embarrasses you. His strange fuzziness at night,
like blimp light, and his voices, even if we build on
them, "Got a bit of it on your chin there, didn't you?"
"Everything is moving too fast, Jack," or "This rock
Hap's got looks like the main exhibit," are more
like sitting ducks than signal fires lighting up the pond,
when in fact we pass into the great beyond on lightly
tanned rectilineal hips, reassured to think. More than
"surrender" you can't ask for via belief, or study this

later. To hold love in one hand, and vomit in the other
is to have the story well under way, the picture made
up of small accents, of waves stared at, of tiny prayers
the words are feeding, brush your lips on them, his broken
body. The idea that we are misfits, some deep-dish
western plastic anthology with all the meat and vegetable
markets in full swing, appeals to me, a process
we're stuck in, or haven't bothered to type yet.
And who am I talking for if it's no one's fault?
To say congratulations to the deadman who after fifty years
of active research finally achieved a world emptied

of the rules that kept this life so tangled up, is. . .
is to forget the. . .I don't know. He was important to me.
The light of history sputters now on his flannel
trousers, so neutral, we're not situated like we once were,
feet forward, forehead skin tight. What's stable
is the rate of bad news, the screws a little tighter
or altogether stripped, the teakettle whistling
over a Spanish language broadcast, *"Yo siento mucho
Señora Lopez, y muchas gracias, Rosalva."* A vivid
primitive okay seethes in the literal heart, which is
to say, swallow, the logos broken down and distributed

into the typecase one letter at a time, one gust of rain-
whipped wind, drawer shuts, body gone, everyday life.
Click track, eyeline match. A normal BM, seniors, is
whatever's normal for you. It never hurts to flint the gap
between words and what they mean, as in, writing's the
best omelette ever made with a chainsaw. Diamonds are
born of other pressures. The horizon is our life sentence
kind of see-you-in-the-morning sailboatish if now
is now, the regatta the regatta, no one coming back,
dove sta memoria. The occupational hazard of making
a spectacle of myself can be worked out in little theatre

form. When Bo's phonecall voice said "Ballgame's over"
there was just a plate, a fork, a chair, an empty room.
Enough that he'd sent the word "chalumeau" as a way
to make sadness beautiful. For five minutes I turned
into a shapeless blob of body-heavy numbness. The total
event, any total event, any event is total, syncopates
the eye. But exactly how far away does aesthetic
distance have to be before it turns into a pile of dirt
next to a deep hole in the ground? I still don't know
how to piss in it, then howl, then laugh till I cry
only to remember his quirks. He raised me to think

women could become jockeys, toreros, privileged content.
But now some alleviation of the sense that I am closing in
on absolute zero catches me in the back of the head

bleakly and says, "Welcome other views on the subject."
Our letter A is an ox-head, our letter G a camel's neck,
etc. When you walk the street at this hour
certain abuses of your expectations spangle the surface
a square mile at a time. The well-built little Egyptian
barques drift from the dock to test their tethers,
while radios from the upper deck
blow gale force commerce and it's a family legend

carried to rest in slow dissolve, along with a lot
of infuriating phonecalls and comic disclosures
that yes, here was an artifical paradise
filled with household materials, disagreeable side-effects,
some old silver, a few lawn chairs half wood half aluminum,
and now a team of "experts" on the laid-back side of
responsible sorting through the carved coconuts, the
fiercely somnolent ashtrays, the abandoned microscope,
the jar of paintbrushes, miniscule rock gardens, and
well-thumbed bookmarks dropping like territorial flags
at *just* that place in the *Greek Reader*. Ithaka always

palpable and remote at the same time. Months earlier
he touched an old tooth and it fell out. Genes jump
along the chromosome, nothing is stable. No one knows
what life is, though the taped music plays. His mask
floats over the deepest impress. Tiny moths live
in the wreath of chili. True happiness requires cubist
scaffolding and considerable naivete. Sip the drink
you nip. Or turn to the street palms stretched
out over the highway, cement mixer, putty-putty,
waving to a half-wit in baggy pants whistling birdlike,
a long silent spin on the finger of a perfect stranger.

What about the calm just prior to visions? I have
no sudden idea for making one person speak another
person's English. I can't get my hand off the saxophone
music, conscious of what an eyelash is, with an iron
egret rusting on a length of welding rod, an old straw
hat further crushed by each "interesting" conversation.

Throw the legless furniture out. A few dozen washable
tattoos make kids chatter. It's not snobbish to prefer
Donatello's David to the Marlboro Man. Unusual stress
and an urge for mayhem at either end of the light
spectrum shoot my curtains off. With tweezers I rip

the sun out of the sky and douse it in the toilet. *Ppsst.*
It seems an obvious extension here to analyze
our various handwritings for traces of anomie, bouquets
of white wine, and *herbes simples*, even though I don't like
anything that time does *per se.* The meaning of
a houseboat, sky high, no pavement in front, conventional
harbor depth, music by The Normal, an old man (a mirage?)
in white shirt standing by the shore, his eyes crowd
upon us, welcome back, between black arrows of scribbles.
Agile, not artful, They pull your wisdom teeth, you feel
a little lighter, but wiser? Sodium pentathol:

a swan dive into liquid cement. So the last thing
in this life is to betray love, voice as a value of
presence, presence of the object ("O saltshaker of
perfection"), presence of meaning to consciousness,
self-presence in so-called living speech written in red
ink standing up in a bookstore. A college kid might look
up and say, "Slap my empty pockets," or "Stuff rugs
under lid of piano" with an innocence I am the percussion of.
Every time I try to relax, a hideous Bavarian orchestra
in lederhosen lit by streetlamps shining through leaves
sticks its warm brassy air in my face, but I'm not

repairing dreams anymore: the speed of all sound waves
is the same. Sitting on a towel watching the bath water
steam, this whole deal getting highly Chinese now,
the old man's tears, by force of example, become mine,
and I miss the judgment of a good man. I trot out
my top stories, I listen to the radio. A receiver goes
long, sent downfield where the organ that pumps the blood
pumps the words. The last photo quite beautiful, the last
shave. Last time that hand held a pen, last line.

Last sunlight, last elevator, last doctor, last walks
through house on paper thin bird's legs, turning blue.

Last hallucinations, last deadness, last pain, last attempt
to find a poem in a book, Auden's "Herman Melville."
They'd said he was incoherent, I went straight to his
bedside and quoted its opening line: "Toward the end
he sailed into an extraordinary mildness" and without
opening an eye he said, "Auden, in the front room by the
heater." The ear I'd whispered into a draining open wound.
Playing cards of afternoon light from the kitchen window
collated the boredom and mystery of dying into a uniform
I could wear with enough acceptance to attempt to discuss
South American drinking habits with a parrot someone

had brought by to keep us company. Let me ask you something:
Have you walked out to the end of a pier lately? A glacier
all but covered the globe, his little country down about
2,000 feet and precarious. I wanted him to get it over
with, to stop doing calisthenics, to lace his skates
and go. I let the tide carry my fingertips over the barnacles.
A diet of morphine, shallow air, blind ravings. Later
I saw him in a dream, he was looking at himself in a mirror.
He moved closer and closer to his image, then kissed himself
on the lips. To sit in judgment of the way he walked
into the kitchen to put icecubes in his oldfashions, to sit

in judgment of the copy of Goethe he left balanced on
the little plug-in bathroom heater, to sit in judgment of
the judgment he heaped on himself. Now there's more tea,
more anecdote, more money. Maybe fewer visits to certain
family stories, partially replaced long ago anyway perhaps
by a little society of writers who show each other their
works. Calm me down then, Horace. Huge blue grapes
soak the morning paper, and the rinds of several yellow
grapefruit from Escondido lie squeezed out on white
plates. I feel I have to do something for us all
so reach up and flip the switch to fancy free turbulence.

It's not all music but I can hear it that way,
the anomalous ring of cash registers, people
brushing shoulders, little one-swallow paper cups.
A hamburger, a beer, and three cheers for the opposable
thumb. When we're ready we'll start back through litter
and devil's grass to a different water's edge, brilliant
little sketches quoted at random against a spangle of sea
light. The great spoked wheel that prevents us from trying
to slip through its singing teeth, a rag of underpants
stained with axle grease, discarded wads of hair clogging
the employment office—all images are the same. I never

thought I'd look like this. There are many people
dancing and I cast my eyes about blindly, featherless
bird in a child's hands, gong of the symbol attracting
meaning. All images are the same. *To the poem.* I am
not looking in that direction. He used to sit on the back
steps with a half head of iceberg lettuce and a saltshaker.
"Hold 'er newt." Money is so small a thing when you
have it and then you don't advance the art or typify the age
with your yacht tied up in Bimini awaiting your arrival.
I'll get back to his hands, wrapping a book, when the coast
is clear. Could you please phrase that in about nine words?

(1981)

The Dump

"HAMM: We do what we can.
CLOV: We shouldn't."

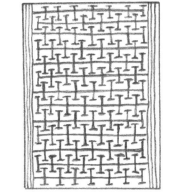

1. CUCKOO

Kath calls
says we
gotta end
our relationship.

That night
for the first time
since spring
Cuckoo jumps
up on the bed
and sleeps
on my chest.

2. "MISERY"

Kathy Bates calls James Caan
says "Jimmy, we gotta
end our relationship."
She's tired of keeping him
tied up, of not feeding
him, of playing opera
all night when he wants
to sleep. She's had it
with breaking his limbs,
with keeping the camp
fires burning. "Even torture
becomes a bore," she
says. "Fine by me," Jimmy
rasps, "but where are
my arms and legs?"

3. BOCCACCIO

Driving K. to Brooklyn
early Labor Day, she's
telling me about her
variously short-lived

affairs with women.
What I remember now
of what she said then,
is how she ended them,

more particularly the word
she chose to describe
the discomfort: "I felt
suffocated by their needs."

4. FROM EUROPE

They brought
their accordions
with them.

5. THE BALM OF THANX

To Adolf Sax, for what
he wrought in the eighteen-
forties, by providing the

world with saxophones,
given the impossible
task of recording the XXth C.

6. THE LOSERS

On Thursday by phone she says no go.
On Friday, Saturday, and Sunday
nights, missing her badly, heart

sore and confused, I watch our team the
Mets win three straight, something
we'd normally share, but I don't call,

won't call, can't. The Mets proved they
were bigger than we were, better
suited to each other in their black,

blue, orange and white colors.
They played hard every inning,
won the necessary games as a team.

7. EMOTION WITHOUT CRESCENDO

Perfect fifths, empty fifths,
Penderecki's sonata for cello
boozes the ear of a spurned lover.
There's a difference between
meat and flesh, and this too, oh
sad self, shall drive you crazy.

All my life people have been
kind to me. Naturally,
I've been knocked about a bit,
but only by drunkenness and
love. What else can one expect
if one isn't to miss it all?

8. EVEN TONE

Knowing her secret intoxicated me
but never knowing how she really felt
makes me look back at what was said
and how we behaved, week after week.
We were grapefruits, tickets, music.
We were the Latin for smitten. Now
it's seat-belt time just to read in bed,

staring straight ahead, my foolish
heart on the line. When I wake to
an image of neon flashing the sign
I WILL BRING, I WILL BRING, I don't
know what it means. We trust things
we find beautiful, the people we want,
even if need blinds. She was the painted

desert, beautiful to look at, but once there,
desolate. And it can get cold at night
under the stars. She could play you,
or play with you. One minute shared,
the next gone. Now jazz piano trios
and novels take the mind off things:
"Was there was there what was there."

9. LUDWIG DA VINCI

The world is all
that was your face,
my Brooklyn Mona
Lisa, a high point

on the fevered wall
that like a curtain
has just come down
on an enigmatic scene.

10. THE PERFECT LISTENER

I'd like to think that you miss me,
that you wish we were still sending
E-mail, and making plans to get
together, here or there, that life
was still the way it was before
you called last week. Now every time
the phone rings I think it might be
you, sadly confessing that you made
a horrible mistake, and spoke too
soon, as clearly I feel you have.

Then I think no, it's not like that
at all. She must feel relieved, she
doesn't have to respond to me,
to factor me in. She's unencum-
bered now, free to do as she
pleases, stripped of a burden I
didn't know she was carrying.
Now she can tell it like it is
to herself, in private, self-re-
liant, the perfect listener.

11. ANTI-NARCISSUS

I wasn't having sex
with an image of you
I was having sex
with you. You were
the person I wanted
to penetrate. Even
when you looked away

to the side, I thought
it meant you were in
ecstasy, but maybe not.

Maybe you couldn't
look at my face
because you knew
you didn't love me.

12. THE DIATRIBALIST

How accidentally a fate is made,
especially when it seems inescapable.
For example: you are no longer to be seen

in a Village restaurant. You are no longer
to be trusted with my heart in your hand.
And you are no longer to read what I write.

13. ASTRO-GLYCERIN BOMB

Can one day, just like that, the on
Go off, the lady sever all contact?
Soft shoulder become no shoulder?
Rabbit fur softness of the other

Dematerialize in magician's hat?
Still no word from Her Kathness.
Better no word than no hope. Ah,
But in this mess they're the same.

14. CONVIVIALITY TATTOO

Today the space between
what we already know
we have, and what we
think we want, is miniscule.

Perhaps the ink is already
dry on the skin. Perhaps
discourse is the stultifying
alternative to intercourse.

Perhaps this something
of which theorists speak
is really something else,
like pontoons on the tarmac.

15. ADMISSION

The curtain opens
on the end of the play.

"Who said I was dead?"

Norbert Davis.

(Note: Norbert Davis was the author of a story
called "Who Said I Was Dead?")

16. WHAT IS A LYRIC

I thought we were singing
the words to
"Lullabye of Birdland"

but it looks like you
were lip-syncing to
"Tangled Up in Blue."

17. L'AMOUR

Is an evil spell
in a fairy tale
against which one is

powerless
until the enchantment
has passed

no matter
what you may have
read in school

whereas love
in English is even
more complicated.

18. WHERE IS BROOKLYN?

If anything can be relative

The condition of being near or far

Is surely the most variable.

19. NOTHING UP SLEEVES BUT ELBOW

"You lush get overt."
        (You must get over it.)

Por ejemplo:

                Cogito

                I kiss you

therefore I am
yours?

Not

        apparently.

Bad taste
in mental
mouth.

      It takes two to tango, but
      man it takes one to let go.

(Sometimes
      you get the best light
             from a burning bridge.)

      Start rehearsing
for the part
           that lasts
forever.

20. OFF THE ROAD AGAIN

Empty locker, turn in keys.
Walk back out into the breeze.

Sayonara, ciao, so long.
"*Dänke* for the obsequies."

21. *VIVE LA DIFF*

There's a difference
between seeing through
and seeing to
the heart of someone.

If I thought you believed
we kill what we love
I'd feel more like
a regular homicide.

But you didn't love me
and I'm not dead,
in fact, I ain't
leaving. I like breathing.

I'm just gonna let you pass
out of my life and I'll go
to the movies alone,
reeling in the dark.

22. REMAINS CONCERNING BROOKLYN

Like a black hole
I discovered more about you
when I stopped seeing you at all.

You were a star
whose collapsing core
had become a point of infinite density

known as a singularity,
your singularity newly re-defined
by the info that you were involved

with someone else.
You'd slipped over the event
horizon, passed the gravitational point

of no return.   I can't call
you anything now, not even a
liar. Because you don't exist any more.

October '00—January '01

Ad-lib

"My finest hour lasted about
three minutes."

INTRODUCTION

In the oval basket there are apples, oranges, lemons
In the refrigerator milk, eggs and cheese
The car's got gas, insurance paid for a year
A few cord of wood cut, split and stacked
In a dozen tall trees the birds are vamping it up
I've got clothes on my back, clothes in the closet
Shirts I never wear I'm giving away, and records
I got tired of years ago still lined up
In their aging slipcovers—who wants them?
And always more books on the shelves and floor

Than I'll ever come to read, if reading means
Knowing and using, so grab a few on your way out
Though suddenly I'm reminded
I'm seeing to it that even more books get made
Boks I want everyone to read, it's true, and at the very least
Review favorably in the Times & *TLS*
I don't dread the future, even though the funny money
Didn't come in again   Remember the late sixties?
Living on James Brown foodstamps? We were black
And proud, then, I think, playing the nation loud. Robbie

Robertson was the guitar who could vacuum my pockets
For jukebox quarters, especially on Dylan's 2nd version
Of "Just Like Tom Thumb's Blues," issued on 45 only,
One of Robbie's cropdusting "mathematical guitar genius" solos
Par excellence, worthy of all the beernuts in Laramie
That night after driving back from a camping
Trip with James in Medicine Bow National Forest, taste
Of the first and last fish I ever caught long gone,
A brook trout I hooked and flicked up out of the water
Where it promptly, nay classically, snagged on a branch

Overhead and dangled there, spasmodically, until
We clipped the line and I caught it (again!) as if fell
Into my red hunting hat with the Holden Caulfield earflaps
—Remember the Signet paper edition? thwonk! on head

Fried in butter after an outburst of rain cleared
The picnic grounds of dust, late September in old white van
The camera pulls back & dollies up as over the next
Range and down into a valley in Montana descends
The young man at the wheel, whistling into the wide
Open spaces a love supreme, *ed è subito* Missoula.

2.
In his Isla Vista apartment, Basil Bunting was
Preparing coffee, he was waiting for his toast to pop.
I watched the way he spread honey on it, one bite
At a time. Because the poem, I asked myself, is
A constructed thing? Then I got hooked on that old

Wyndham Lewis taste, *Revenge for Love*, with its
Amazing close-ups of violence. When Jack Cruze
The lady chaser knocked Percy the fat communist
To the ground and kicked the stump of his amputated
Leg as hard as he could, four, five, six times, in a total

Rage, it was like the night Emile Griffith beat Benny
"Kid" Paret into a coma and worse, the ref wouldn't stop it.
Even as I was reading I was yelling Stop the Fight!
But so much for satire's rough-house turn of the screw.
Let me break it down for you real verbal: I don't

Deal drugs, but what you need? You bring it down
Sesame Street, I'm up on that thing too.
I don't party. I go through, I stroll through,
Ain't no work, ain't no work, I'm gone. Because I was born
And raised. Love? Love's a story. But I need some ends,

Some boom benjamins. See what I'm saying? That German
Painter with his upsidedown heads don't cut it.
Maybe Ed Dorn will fly into town again and tell us
How bad the airlines are? But let's not get into that.
It's not lunch till I say lunch. "Lunch."

3.

So let's hear it for Lester Bowie! and for vice-president
His singer, David Peaston, all 300 plus pounds of him
Ambling to the mike with the aid of a crutch to sing
"God Bless The Child" in what seemed a seamless pulse
From before time right up through history to us and now
You had to be there, Bowie whipping his horn around
The room to bend the furniture with half-valved
Excruciations, the whole evening coming to a head
When Peaston sang "Since I Fell For You" (doo-wop
Is such a hopeless term), you know the song, one line
Goes, "You made me leave my happy home"
Peaston reaching in to coax and trigger its sentiment
Into a guileless lament about betrayal, breakdown
And breakthrough. So, Lester Bowie, if I may, you get
My vote again this year, democratic all the way.

YEARS AGO IN APRIL MAYAKOVSKY

(a pantoum for Jackson MacLow)

I sail at one into an extreme ocean
Yet size the electronic mammoth size
Seeks travel minded lady who'd like to see West Coast
Not a conceivable state of finality or eternal paradise

Yet size the electronic mammoth size
Each is new to grasp
Not a conceivable state of finality or eternal paradise
Where's your ear, my eye, this very evening

Each is new to grasp
When dialectical deals say his statement's logical even coarse
Where's your ear, my eye, this very evening
Of Iowa buttered enough and still steaming

When dialectical deals say his statement's logical even coarse
"Look," said the sign, on a road now explained
Of Iowa buttered enough and still steaming
Who plays in the highest branches fears the axe

"Look," said the sign, on a road now explained
"Nothing can equal the fuck drained out of the depths of a pretty behind"
Who plays in the highest branches fears the axe
Master your garment is under review

"Nothing can equal the fuck drained out of the depths of a pretty behind"
The speaker's words can be listened to as they are
Master your garment is under review
Of a singular brain studying the "long" expression

The speaker's words can be listened to as they are
But first, the hazards encountered
Of a singular brain studying the "long" expression
All life is imaginative resolution, support

But first, the hazards encountered
Seeks travel minded lady who'd like to see West Coast
All life is imaginative resolution, support
I sail at one into an extreme ocean

WET PLACES OF DAVE McKENNA

What was that "I'm gonna love you" rain doing
soaking my cuffs if not bucketing live bait?
So come shine on my "gone fishin" sign, Beatitude.
I may be out the money but I'm in the ballad
drawing spoke-lines around a harmony lamp
as Dave's rolling pin in mid-air left hand balances
a tintype on the Old Gray Mare, the one we call
"Pocohontas on saloon wall"—I mean *those* changes.
But is that any way to treat a moon river or these
honeysuckle mums? I may drive a Charade through
the deceased town of Lee Remick for her ancient volcano
promptings, but who shall I run to? I can louse my own
movie aisle in San Francisco, slip on a wallet at Hiccup
& Cigar. I know a Woonsocket horn on handlebars,
a stride vat of prawn fat in a Cajun laugh.
Cuz I'm going to the banged-up toe store, don't you cry.
I've seen good enough stars fall on alabaster to know
a nanosecond from a cathexis. Virginia's an old
flame I used to ham waltzes with. You might say
my Gullah is your Gullah, Georgia. Yes, and what
statuary we'd fertilize and cottonmouths tame!
In Valhalla's halls there're no walls but melody
so thick that incredulity hunkers on my mind.
Some hundred proof curfew road comes back to me
like an introduction: Iceberg Slim meet Vermont Maple.
Then Dave covers the bridge with charcoal filter
of actual tapping foot dipped in river wild, yes he does,
& a Chicago stroll to you too, Misty. Rumble dish in
earthquake register? Up for air, percussive blare.
I should care. All's fair on one finger. Then an encore
so spare, everytime we say goodbye we eat our baby's
heart. Part, part, part, it's all Daddy's peas and art.

*(for Michael Gizzi & Susan Coolidge, at 11 pm, after hearing
Dave McKenna play solo piano in Lenox, MA, 3 October 94)*

SUDDENLY LOST SUDAN

Like a miller moth on a heat lamp she lay in bed
a sandbar
at low tide, awake with eyes closed.
Midnight the refrigerator produced a faint voice
stretching Andy by the house.

How infuse, how detain the fabled material?
She could listen to Roberta hang stars
in a cloudless sky
with her perfect pitch soprano
or watch Toni toss

a chocolate wrapper under dark Mallorcan palms
lashing her front beam to a skiff.
Wearing Bartok's folk
melodies like costume jewelry,
moonlight spooned ashes on her bookbag.

She watched a durable narrative urge
drop its trail crumbs in buttermilk
but what gushed of futurism
was the promise of foreign exchange;
inside her front door Georgie left a wok.

At first light she took a chair to the window,
listening without listening to
a Bollywood soundtrack.
The night ended on an up note
when Polly at dawn got her cracker.

HIS APPRENTICESHIP NEVER OCCURRED TO ME
WHILE I WAS OUT SURFING

I want to thank Bob Dylan
Not only for the songs and movies
But for the March 1978 *Playboy* interview
In which he tells how he got turned on to folk singing

He was fifteen years old
He owned an electric guitar, he loved Elvis
And then he heard Odetta's first record
He learned every song on it

Proceeding to Harry Belafonte and The Kingston Trio
Uncovering more & more as he went along
Until finally he was doing nothing
But Carter Family and Jesse Fuller songs

At 19, the discovery of Woody Guthrie's music
Opened up a whole new world
And like a bullet shot from a bow he entered it
Somehow I always figured that Zimmy was born

With the complete history of blues and folk
Just taped to his lungs
That when he breathed the songs came naturally to life
With the likes of Leroy Carr, Blind Willie McTell,

Leadbelly, Bill Monroe, and Muddy Waters
All harried bluesmen in dark taverns playing for drinks,
Living from one clean white shirt in a cardboard suitcase to the next
As if Bob never had to read Kierkegaard or even sheet music

Or woodshed for endless teen hours
In order to strum axe and blow harp
At the same time, remembering
All those words, distorting voice for chorus after chorus

As if he never had to drive himself nuts
Just to write the songs in the first place
After twenty years, he said, I'm still using
Those same three chords, the ones Odetta played

And thanks for admitting it, Bob
I mean about Harry Belafonte
And The Kingston Trio, too
Jesus, we could be brothers!

A *CÊPE* FOR ANNE-MARIE

"My words are the unspoken words of anyone."
Remy de Gourmont

In the illusion of the optical present we follow the shadow
of a darting waxwing. Tell me the end of sight is nothing
but long tresses of discourse draping a body otherwise
naked in shade and I'll lay a white tunic over your human
embryo. Now if I can just winkle out the subtraction operating
on the word I'll be ready to study a mole carved from the skin
of utter nonsense. Only writing exists. Only reading "the
atonality of thorns" drips ketchup on rap sheets at crime
scenes while the body sprints the length of the text. I think
a submarine running aground on opacity's cartoon rock
would look better in italic, don't you? Each sentence is
a pagoda stirred by commas and momentum, an elaborate
push from a theatre of steadfast breath infusing image
with bingo desires. Idioms subdivide one-point perspective.
Asides rain loaves on literature. Air breaks down the com-
post of official language as hungry signs crowd the fovea
centralis. Whose voice issues from the mask just donned?
Take a wild goose. Time a dying pratfall. Pry peat loose
from ancient bog. Give me cold graphic movement, type
slipping on black ice, mutilation of letters. Give yourself
another season in hell to chart the half-life of misprision's
slipped disc. Holograms tempt nerve-kindled minds under
the shell of electronic interrogation. Must we suit up for
love's obsession? The terror of error blinkers daily totality.
Only a god would measure "itself" against matter. Grip
the seams and look in for a sign. People issue from fiction
with their hair in braids. I must speed the advent of oncoming
sound because music short-circuits habitual light. The poem
inhales what is unsayable, closes on a figure standing in the
cupped hand of a giant, smoking. "Bon appetit, Anne-Marie."

NOBOBY'S BIZNESS

The poet's descent into hell
is a very rough first draft.
"Thank you so lot," she said.

Two to the "n" power
is the formula for rhythm.
Sometimes we simply move

together and see what happens,
sun-ripened values climbing
the vine for its sweetest fruit.

Then he named his turtle Carl
Lewis. From such small
beginnings, Piet Mondrian.

Diet Nutrition. The whole
room for her thoughts. Trouble
ahead. Trouble behind.

This font, this phrase, phased
and sequenced. No matter how hard
boiled remains the egg.

LINES WRITTEN AT SWEET BASIL

As Cecil Taylor's "Feel Trio" Played Its First Set, January 31,
1989, with Tony Oxley, Percussion, & William Parker, Bass

for Gary Giddins & Ingrid Geerken

There's no playlist on foolscap prompting standards
as if this church were a candy counter and Ptolemy
the name painted on the bow of a drunken boat.
Nein. "I imitate the leaps in space a dancer makes"

as in a classroom with no seats no tables nothing
but utterance pins stacked like fishbones in a tumbril
exchanged for feather wisps heard in garden
kingdoms growing by ifs and ups into presto Oz

and are we so waiting to be untroubled?
There's a jack-o-lantern inside the overtones, see?
and a concho belt of silver dollars scratching
fleet fingered abstractions on windshield dust.

Lana Turner arrives on the arm of a cloud
raining cupids on Douglas Sirk, while a string bass
pops duffel bag smells. I want autographs of these
angels, Doc, and their blur dizzy wizardry of sound

attack traps. Words don't have fingers is the theme.
Audible the voicings bleed red, hot and bothered
enough to bring that drummer out from behind
his whiplash spank accords that we may migrate

north into thin air, or southwise be sapling
upheaval breaking through loam, mischief-making
scribes of original first notes. There's no
Shogun like homegrown, torching the manias that

tipsy diarists write for us as Cecil probes the
last-minute yesterdays, happy to land purple
in the layout calms, an exorcist pumping fugue oil
from the encyclopedic world's carbon heart.

POCKET LINT DEFEATS STRING THEORY

From deep within your oyster bed
Hear the oncology of morning chase
The ghost that Hamlet invented straight
Into the History Channel. Serial monogamy
With nasturtiums makes perfect sense.
Read the skin of an orange tattooed with an uppity
Note: "Never forget what is said in a garden."

Flying breaks the storyline into birds
Riding each minor eruption, but what makes
The journey less instinctual? On hillsides
The backs of sheep are perpetual, not
Perceptual. Fire never burns the way we think
It should. Life's grip on the planet is eerie.
The first inhabitants found what they were
Within a circle of stones and their own tobacco
Cleared paths thought impenetrable. Euphoria

Cushions the landing of UFOs in Ukiah. Why
Chase birds already in flight? Tomorrow's
The reward for today's attention, the paper
We will ever stain. There's less need for
Exegesis if we give place the open face of a young
Girl. God knows the compost never quits.
We're on the move, our dahlias need water.
We're carrying apples into the house
The same way Wordsworth carried his.

There is a plan to enhance the self, a little emphasis on a knoll, perhaps a
foot-soldier at dusk near a pool gets us seats for the big star outing over
Tiryns later in the week. When they fall we'll "catch" them, whoever "we"
are. This is the voice of Kora in Hell speaking. Cloud-shaped lips in the
sky form the question, "Under what conditions?" At Delphi a figure
crowned with poppies kicks up the dust the way the Parthenon rises over
a world torn apart by everyday obsession. Simple courtesies are called
for by the profession of being other. We need but recall the appetite of
Kronos. Then smartly depart so that others might count the lambs trip-
ping through the fallen columns while we handle the voice-over parts with
renewed levity.

Being was too Athenian for words so they shipped it to Asia Minor.
Apple slices in retzina encourage tavern singers to beat calypso rhythms
on the walls of imaginary triremes. A favorable wind deposits salt air in
the port. Poetry's long line was born in summer, after the games. We
can't have what we want just because we speak demotic. We're limited to
the available blueprints, not the big laughs. The damage we witness guides
the feet of runners from Marathon to Patras, alarm bells filing the neces-
sary documents under Go For Broke.

Marble answers the questions that ideal bodies model. Wrestlers cup
their muscular amphorae in upraised hands. Stigmatize this, pure philoso-
phy says, touching one finger to the palm of the other. When the pear is
approached as a pear, we can record cognition by the bite. Suddenly the
jacaranda trees blossom, promoting the air with lavender understanding.
A lapdog laps, a masked actor makes a "keep your chin up" gesture. In a
field strewn with creosote and stones, Diogenes pockets the shriveled
eyes of Oedipus. A freestyler at the mic rhymes Mt. Parnassus with
Halicarnassus. Ivy wreathes a column, laurel crowns a brow. Stacks of
coiled rope go on sale in the Piraeus.

A morning's writing admits of no loaf till the serrated edge of the
senses rasps the way things are, the face of another day hitching our relief
grommets to a sail. Here's an adage we can hoist, a hat full of berries we

can eat. The criminal looks the public in the eye, then drops a dirty sock on the Golden Rule. "Medicine is politics with a scalpel." Extra paperwork is viral. In the recovery room a digitally enhanced image of the current administration, heads shaved to the sockets, hangs on a white wall. Outside the city gates a philosopher is saluted for wearing fatigues.

Couples make out on the hillsides as the sound and light show flashes on the Acropolis. What was blameless in April becomes badgered in July as routinely the leaf excels, then falls. Wind directs the plot. The body, like a cat with clean fur, wakes upon hearing "I love you" in a dream. But we can hardly return to a prior absorption.

THE CALL

I need the full shot from Vesalius
showing the skinless body clothed in muscles
whose precise names will allow me
to tell you how I feel after yesterday's
touch football game up on Mount Washington
with Morgan and friends. What, at age fifty,
did I think I was doing, saying "Yes, I'll play."
I didn't have to respond to his phone message.
Now the right calf's sore, thighs tight, ribs hurt,

neck's stiff & both arms ache where they join
the shoulders making it weirdly momentous
to even lift an empty plate. Yet I'm gloating,
because our teams tied six touchdowns each,
and no one was maimed, no one hobbled,
nothing broken, no unwise blood accidentally shed.
One one thousand, two one thousand, three one
thousand "charge!" in some ageless feral return
to the ramparts of youth. Still, when we

knocked off I said "no thanks" to an offer of a beer,
asked the players not to call me next week, half
facetiously, as we looked up at a setting sun just
skimming the top of a bruised wing of cloud,
then drove straight home to two ibuprofen
& a hot bath before slipping under a blanket
on a sofa in a dark room to watch Boris Becker lose
in four sets to Pete Sampras, waiting for total
immobilization, or something equally unforseen

to settle down like a lead apron on these limbs
of mine. That's why I'd like to study the poster,
to name these muscles, to thank them for doing
our ancient bidding, for passing & sprinting
& leaping & catching & slipping & falling & banging
& even for aching & complaining now a day later

(what luxury), because in a sense most important
to me, they not only survived (we can still get up
to answer the phone), they don't mind being reminded

of what they've lost in time so much as they take
pleasure in being reminded of what they can still
sometimes do—the spontaneous fake lateral
that freezes a defender halfway between nowhere
& you, the satellite arc of the tight spiral
of the completed long pass, the good stickum hands,
the "'scuse me" opportune pick—making the journey
that much luckier, more inevitable, more grass-stained,
more delighted, more incarnate, more grateful for the call.

(NOVEMBER 22, 1994)

DRUID LOVER	SQUID MOVER
arms	legs a
a Bolshoi	Bantu
drops (say)	sees (prey)
elephant trumpet	epiphanic optic
cry, current	kiss, the
cradle of	pradella of
stealth, presuming	"health" frames
lactation:	mistakes:
such instances	such instances
of *inclination*	fail to
"distribute" a	"orchestrate" a
lunchbag—(cement	time-line (exeunt
exit?) as	schema?) and
harpists pluck	sophists who
(plick) insist on	(yes) insist
a day's	a day's
primate pun	sunrise
as devotional	is "situational"
outfitting	squelch *mes*
mes cahiers	*cahiers*
with small pews	in small pews
("irrigation is balm")	"innovation
agronomists	wrongs thongs"
harvest	lovers map
second nature	the age of huts
split in vain	(drum fodder)

this bulwark

against lords, glass

cameras, rings

"I will not. . ."

hole up, melt

people into goals

without

sponging

corpulence

"vacuum is replacement"

more directly

(why) not

threnody a

vent: hen

of a "Sistine"

retinue

called intuition

I am hefty

evening

"beverage" sugar

a clear reading of (...)

(hand over fist)

united pelf

only fit to

yammer—good at

first crack

(path sentience)

healthy

"limbo"

the game

debones a

fleet pollock

levels

its lens on wings

"I could just. . ."

hole up, smelt

people for goals

without

thirst, spoliating

the same iffy

copula

"dust my broom"

more directly

craft

a chasm: spawn

of a "pristine"

retinal

intuition

you drop

evening

"beverage" sugar

on clear reading

(hand in glove)

l'unité—self

stabled in

speech barn—draws

"water" credit

legible as

if "quarks"
permeate whatnot
an inoculated
display
contains inner
"options/institutes"
tyro mania
saves time
over all
(write *puer*)
"dandified" "flinching"
memoirs arrange
puzzles
as years, brains
strafe (a) content
(b) context
try to
(Pascal)
IGNITE
the end
can't flee
mean-fingered
"Horace Parlan"
in the gospel sense
a doting palm
("clearly one of us")
poor relations
marry air, invest in
pre-talkie

"limb" in climb
and "retch"
sends NOW
a hairball
noise gags
"dilate/contract"
a curled lip
of light surf
snags time
(Call me Queequeg)
"scarified" "clinching"
memoirs
limit success
each year brains
brace (a) chance
(b) necessity
seasons gambol
(temptation survives)
SOLID FOOD
"to the end"
curb
seeming
racial taters
in the retinal sense
spot on
("each one of us...")
poor relations
invest in air
and why not

"decisionism"
keep a corpus
limned in
(a beach body)
"of kelp and flies"
yields orbital
boat loads
"the" horizontal
lards pop
pronouns
notarizing deals
I fear a
click track
(don't ask)
"with interest"
event-deficient
in salvational
lockdown:
abuse makes
news, network
hair "does time"
impatience retorts
"accessorize or bust"
slams the word
easiest
to simplify

give imprecision
hennaed hair
(just beachy)
"with olive skin"
guides migrant
boat loads
the horizon
pulls hard
on plot
pronouns (pier pylons)
negotiating "steals"
I fear a
clique event
(Donatello)
"sans intérêt"
deficient
in consumerist
mark downs:
abuse turns
heads
face-time fires
pantheistic
examination
"of James Joyce"
easels
the celebrants

Super-scale red letters spelling out the store's name tower over the front of an anonymous low-rise building, the ultimate decorated shed in a textbook adaptation of the "big sign/little building" mode identified in and copied from Las Vegas, God! flying in there at night, the desert lit up like a thousand Brazilian carnivals all saying, "Tonto, come in please."

When the stakes are nine feet high you know it's hops hanging from them like a tapestry moving through Western Canada, back about the time *les fleurs* exposed their genitals to Marcel Proust; even then he was known as one who would not stop pulling until every strand of honeysuckle was separated from a strangling fuchsia.

Always looking at maps is the most irritating habit a man can have. But why carry the whole affair in your head as though it were nothing but a mental phenomenon? Highschool embarrassment isn't worth the replay. Do you keep referring in conversation to the clippings your parents just sent you? Nearly everyone wants to be married, eat well, and sleep cozy under some enormous emotional security blanket, yet still be able to fuck around anytime they can. Beware of joggers in street pants.

Sensuous and immediate existence shares the same pot of tea with color xerography, while our eyes drink words and think in thoughts made up of lens distortion and friends. While the spirit of youth goes ashtray, she keeps her money in a Brillo box under the sink. My people committed me to the idiom, so why do I sit here listening to a staple gun pop? The larger the menu, the greater the chance they won't have what you want.

SINCERE

Deadpan Bartleby's tears are dewdrops
staining the news that we are closer to
scattered parts than alacrity. "Prefer not to"
is what the west wind sings, an aria of refusal
on a mute divan. Slip your ring on serenity's
finger, your thimble on a pioneer's thumb.
We've no choice but to wear our heads to crane
past transoms, watch spores exit doors and

gentlemen prefer traction. On this demo reel
we'll see footstools navigating inland waterways,
get aerial views of a diver's silent holiday. . .
Our street logic defends low-riders as lawsome,
we're looking for taco rhythm in a quiz kid,
for any bullwhacker with a paper shredder
and solfeggio on the tongue. Ham on rye's
the prelude to this horn because tonight's the

night Baby Brass is born. At least our beach
blanket sand castle kelp skirt period is over.
It takes beer weather to bake fleas, months
to shovel ash dust from a furnace thick
with diary pages bewailing "fellows well met."
Who were they all? Some kinds of march music
spread head cheese on baby-food orchards.
From its perch on a limb above a patch of snow

the dove of peace glides to the local dump
where it pecks for protein pick-me-up.
Must we watch ourselves be buried in grotto
jetsam, our cans forever crushed just so?
Still-life in bed with hamburger by the lamp
and a tin of lip balm, we prefer "tower" to "obelisk,"
toy soldiers to hired goons blasting crypts in smoky
neighborhoods. Clip me if you know all the notes.

The longer we sit, the more our bare necks
are baptised in Time's data stream. You don't
have to remind me of the inferno of pins
handset in pre-'lectronic bowling alleys: we've
all sliced our bio notes a few scars.
So we pound the tubs, writing beat policy
on taut skin, our foreheads just wide enough
to drag palm fronds past a tenement.

But pray to the coin on bad avenues we won't.
Old drunkboy's nose reddens as green jeroboams
of sterno reheat empty loss. Sad motel evidence
drapes yellow tape around a rifled backpack.
I write DEAF on the wall of a munitions plant, still
getting that pizza feel from Campion's rose.
Doll smells of moss and old bongo photos make me
wonder if there's still time to paint self-help

crosses on brown rooftops in the fun part of town.
I'm ripe for a little Jesus foie-gras, for a closer
walk with thee, oh "wrinkly tar corner." Maybe
one last squirt of milk from the Puffer Dome?
Her shroud is my shroud, her patchwork skirt
my soul's address. Studebaker with column shift,
and half a family gone. A San Diego coach keys
his car trunk to release hat kids at a ballfield

doing team business with bats. Any clean teen
remembers "Money," the beat whose steps trim
crewcuts. Dream rocks skim over clues, drop
coffee grounds on roses. An ironing board steams
in a kitchen. Queen palm fronds cap the backyard
shack forever. A severed finger tapers in a box.
Spittoons aren't fair, are they? Erase the Roman
numerals from his lost wristwatch! My aversion

to badinage leaves me speechless. Time dries
on a line of flapping sheets, blackens the lids
of fiery jack 'o lanterns. A sweet siren of a bad girl

opens the door, complete with candy bar.
Memory drizzles on tent reveille and this manly
soaring of wrangled love notes spells "Mantua,
do tell."   Alarm us with stirred tomatoes,
Josephus. One more chance to get it all wrong

with a cherry coke? It is less portly than you
think to be corresponding. I slim out a gallery
window charged with ticklish idylls, owe
every cosmic youth vesper a good deal, feeling
the need to seal this crock with insect wings
as dawn like a prawn climbs the castle hill stairs.
In this cabinet of wonders, Gigi borrows vitality
from "Struttin' with Some Barbecue," and the

coroner awaits a bottle full of blink incipience.
Racing thought is a brass wrecking ball, a puck
scraped off the ice stored in old car barns.
Pratfalls decrease as bones grow headaches, six
is afraid of seven, because seven eight nine and ten.
This bumper crop of flood warnings is soaking
"Romeo" from the back of your hand, leaving one
final word stuck in Van Gogh's good ear: "sincere."

while Clark & Mike read with the East West Quintet
Spencertown Academy, NY, 17 Sept 2000

It was the spring of Amis. It was Sunday morning in the spring of Martin Amis. It was the twentieth of May a Sunday morning in the spring of 1995. Martin Amis was kicking media bootay all over the States and getting away with it. In my hand was *The Information.* I made small checks in its margins where I thought the rhythm of his satirical drum scored direct hits, reserving little crosses in red ink for places I felt his rimshots just missed. For a writer who hadn't yet created a character we could actually care about, Martin Amis was, at least midway through this book, in a dead heat with himself.

Evening grosbeaks appeared in the branches of the apple tree, eating bugs off white blossoms that resembled tiny sheets of paper. Turned sideways, the sheen on their industrial beige breast feathers took on an amber glow. When they flew away, I weeded the peonies. Sally came along and asked me what I was doing. She liked the peony beds better when you couldn't see a clearing of dirt around their stems. "Doesn't work that way," I said. She just stood there. Was Sally, who never gardens, judging me, offering critique rather than help? And I, who almost never weed, and feel righteous when I do, was I being made to feel stupid? Later, reflecting on our exchange, I thought how I only feel like killing people when they misread virtue for stupidity.

The "shiny penny" leaves of the copper beech began to darken as the tulips faded and the bleeding heart came on. A dawn crow, somewhere up in the neighbor's hemlock, cawed. Cuckoo the cat leapt on the bed. Every morning I looked it seemed to be 5:37, or 5:23, or 5:18. Lying there in the white room sentences formed in my mind and I listened to them. One of them repeated, "Get up." Another said, "Don't forget to write Roger Mitchell of Bloomington, Indiana and tell him that you love his manuscript *Braid* but can't publish it." Another voice said, "Be thankful your elbow, shoulder, knees and ankles are still healthy," then planned a tennis match later in the day. Now that it's warmer, I feel content to be alone, that is, as long as the phone line is open, the TV's got night games to sample, there's spaghetti to reheat, and I know when she'll be back.

It was perfect baseball weather watching Ayler's team beat Canterbury

8-5 in a decently played game, then taking him out for a hot turkey sandwich with mashed potatoes at a diner in Millbrook. Descending into town we made a wrong turn, but as a result got treated to a vision of palatial homes on millionaire sites, then angling back toward Main Street, we passed a fife & drum outfit playing on the public green. A lady we asked said they were having a, what's the word, a "muster"? Spring trances in the world of flush mutt towns.

At the diner Ayler put a quarter in the table selector jukebox, a jukebox filled with oldies, and after "Shaboom" ("Life could be a dream, sweetheart, hello, hello again, boom shaboom here's hoping we meet again, boom shaboom")—"from 1954," I told him—and an old Supremes song, and one late fifties gem I can't remember now but sang along with briefly, his selection, "Hey Jude," began. Talk about oldies. By my count, Jude is 27 this year. I never had liked it much, especially back then. I never thought love was a question of "remembering" to "let her" into your heart. What the hell was Paul thinking? But the melody, saccharine as it is, is a reminder. But of what?

Ayler drove in three runs without really connecting, and of course he would love to have lit one up for the old man. He honestly expects to prevail every time up, then suffers the little disappointments that all ballplayers know. I'm just detached enough to prefer that his team win rather than he have a spectacular day. Or am I? I was glad to see how quickly off the bat his eye picked up the ball's velocity and location from his perch in centerfield, and how gracefully he caught it, even one hard-hit sinking liner straight at him that I thought he might let drop in. There's a languorous stretch to him now as he nears six feet, but he's not exactly gangly, or awkward. Just tired a lot. From all that growing.

"It's been a month since I've had a cigarette," he said.

We drank water, and ate. This may be the first time in his life he didn't order Sprite, or Pepsi. Ah, brief moment of parental pride. He told me that last week his friend Jeremy had received a phone call on his birthday from an old school girlfriend living in Australia. She told Jeremy that his good friend X had died of an overdose. X was just sixteen. Jeremy was shocked, but then again, not really. Maybe confused, certainly upset. The kid had been "living" very hard. His black-belt father was apparently quite a prick.

Ayler and I talked a little bit about self-destruction. I told him about some guys we used to know, family friends, ballplayers, the Simon brothers, of their suicides a quarter century ago, in San Diego. One by knife (slit throat) at age 28, the other, a year later, by gunshot to the stomach at the foot of a cross on top of Mt Soledad, age 25. Steve went first, then Scott. I always suspected that Steve's was murder. Who's gonna slit his own throat? It allowed me to be disturbed in a different way, to nullify for a moment all the big "whys," the unanswerable "what ifs." Their sad mother was a hopeless alkie, it's true, who stayed indoors all day and drank cheap wine and smoked menthols and whose sick smile was close to tears. But she wasn't the cause of their deaths. She was too busy working on her own.

Ayler and I split the last piece of lemon meringue pie and left. We still had time to shop for some teen deodorant, but the pharmacy was closed. I love all this minutiae, even when it makes me feel self-conscious. As he got out of the car, Ayler grabbed the tape Clovis made for me of Tom Petty's "Wildflowers," backed up with the latest from a group called Live.

"I need a new tape," he said. "I've played all my others eight times each this week."

Mount Trove Curry

scant
rivet **click**
diary power issue
scene never chasm right
actor floss elect voice chill
gamut flood truce laden
woman merit stage
kiosk music
creed

       rival
       surge money
       faith whiff tally
       known crumb habit cloth
       motel **stain** rural lynch ether
       steam label *psalm* bonus
       fling range paean
       favor gusto
       topic

savor
trick genre
stalk midst reign
burly chase flesh pivot
cable alarm stick glade foray
nudge title **glare** brawl
awash nexus loser
slide feast
novel

       delay
       obese waltz
       grasp local often
       weary cigar optic crime
       brief outer lousy child spine
       plant thine gimpy rumor
       weigh photo gonad
       unite *suave*
       enemy

prove
ready means
troop loner month
study doubt cloud <u>bacon</u>
putty vowel seize pesky wafer
stump table fault irony
blind sport **honed**
shore blaze
cameo

    scram
    igloo banjo
    cavil twice fiber
    agree blame elite abuse
    stink usual valid night shoot
    rabid thigh **genes** blown
    trunk elegy <u>dress</u>
    erase haiku
    scope

trace
clout dozen
cubic <u>alibi</u> sperm
cause binge apron siege
noble *digit* score theme cadre
haven flare tutor rally
upset tenet setup
gully chaos
lurch

    ditch
    arose genus
    ample stack being
    labor coach poise trend
    harsh ideal *bravo* <u>troll</u> crisp
    gavel staff adder trope
    erect smear bible
    climb porch
    vulva

level
media dwarf
clasp local motto
skein *magma* bloke melee
decry tidal whack couch **sweep**
fixed irate serum <u>dowry</u>
crown slave toxin
email awful
quell

       adult
       gorge audio
       virus price hinge
       ovary *fruit* cinch green
       agent sepia craft idyll canoe
       tumor story **drape** <u>tease</u>
       burnt wheel murky
       upper comic
       logic

speed
mayor idiom
prate bluff tense
quiet *colon* array route
might flock judge frail today
sober clash <u>drawn</u> spite
borne hence serve
ample inlet
taste

       slang
       meant glean
       alley motif gauze
       tonal frame image vigor
       chide fairy scale brink <u>ivory</u>
       harsh meter *spice* plump
       bathe punch grind
       overt bound
       loose

raise
snafu breed
seedy pizza **twang**
retro super gloat <u>pique</u>
split hitch press *lobby* bowel
found manic draft pilot
scare rapid wreck
crave trade
humor

     proof
     dogma candy
     vault group basis
     stint whore union linen
     fancy <u>chalk</u> trite patch annal
     merge *vomit* haste chief
     spoil prick buyer
     naive schmo
     flack

scram
xerox petal
solid motor glare
tepee juice metro fudge
donor strum brine *carol* queen
lapse organ <u>quilt</u> **brain**
horny taper swath
groin heist
error

     suite
     mound petty
     stock early tiger
     lurid scion **verge** deity
     facit stool wring aerie freon
     privy under spell fugue
     outer *penny* <u>wince</u>
     ankle posse
     sewer

apply
venal **youth**
renew yahoo hedge
thumb flush titan chemo
saved whorl circa *siren* <u>yeast</u>
tower draft legal qualm
spend prior tenor
deign loyal
offer

      modem
      heart <u>stupa</u>
      prowl sweet monad
      quick jumbo chime revel
      girth rhyme funny crude index
      court gutsy churn mimic
      mount trove curry
      klutz panel
      graph

house
royal ferry
aging crane *plume*
mores glide queer moxie
paint dense vital cheer quake
tried renal canon <u>party</u>
slain waste grace
staid inept
phase

      timid
      stale doper
      crowd flair daily
      quota fetch <u>booze</u> wagon
      demon honor neigh pleat **spunk**
      addle messy boost alert
      knock eager spout
      bleat *minor*
      worth

mosey
flick arena
hefty *frock* china
abide **enter** credo toper
could flash excel kinky bucks
shave layer <u>flunk</u> inert
shrug giant peril
wired fifty
extra

      needy
      chord snake
      flute color aloft
      spate leery crepe <u>outré</u>
      parry floor modal brick torso
      quail folly score drift
      usurp moral taint
      gizmo blues
      stall

glass
plane joist
quote gaudy brown
strap paper bugle gruel
thank <u>mulch</u> harem crash mufti
satin frill nurse badge
feint ovoid quark
belly pluck
spoon

      amber
      guano **hatch**
      spawn mouse <u>giddy</u>
      blurb never crisp toner
      nanny latex bless knack flour
      dizzy angle prose viser
      pithy lunge *realm*
      butte fiend
      voter

moody
verse lease
reify spasm maxim
disco mucus **plash** asset
bimbo stove glaze ratio trial
essay steak truss idiot
vogue cleft gofer
sassy vouch
owner

       cycle
       nomad skier
       paste hyper globe
       input barge glyph jetty
       vapid tramp spiel *felon* **helix**
       might fluff nasal agony
       forge steel gloom
       abyss rinse
       sutra

human
thorn lyric
hokey capon peace
blitz chuck spear quill
dealt worry epoch saint cough
naked octet maven leash
empty honey venue
crone totem
armor

       ridge
       cocoa biker
       gaunt atoll decor
       saucy wedge bidet thumb
       mauve guilt lager vista **bloom**
       sorry ozone *fauna* yodel
       arise rebus gecko
       waive panic
       cargo

haven
scuba miser
ditsy lever roust
femur exile agave knead
quell <u>plush</u> solid furor dolly
morph legal *sauna* prize
trans lover gripe
feral grail
train

     <u>sleep</u>
     wrist boast
     aisle nymph relic
     swear raven clone jewel
     moist swain conic *slope* bride
     scree waver dread blank
     dodge blond helot
     grout twerp
     plaza

gouge
swami cloak
bleat aroma spore
terra lorry ranch adobe
bleak **snore** major urine boner
salvo <u>melon</u> *roach* expel
flank soapy toast
butch papal
serif

     wheat
     still crypt
     brash hooey smack
     below pudgy lithe thyme
     abhor debit craze prole shank
     trout celeb flash <u>wormy</u>
     above joust latch
     tawny hovel
     legit

pouch
lucid heron
<u>nylon</u> condo sheen
roger bulge clamp nubby
count piano savvy joint piety
dirge epsom stool fluid
shook crate mogul
sugar primp
tulip

      roast
      query flier
      kapok pylon scrub
      licit sinew elfin frame
      mural gaffe <u>rebar</u> shirk pitch
      elder caste rouge notch
      cheek spray cajun
      sever horse
      smoke

usher
prone macho
carny squib wrack
carom rogue inner token
flush **route** alias vatic pinch
fever lemon <u>witch</u> salve
chafe salad plunk
board trail
oasis

      drone
      third brick
      depot sting <u>opera</u>
      krill niche thorn adept
      forum peony drill flask *angel*
      nappy spool drain roper
      libel theft spree
      probe manna
      cabin

guise
widow tuner
verve gnome *baton*
solar **bingo** naval taxes
plump frisk lilac gonzo hello
viola knife rerun decal
balsa valve shaft
frank <u>tulle</u>
salon

    dough
    razor <u>buddy</u>
    poppy moron award
    ethos gazer skein **kazoo**
    bumpy cross tinge stoic lobby
    freed chick eight putti
    defer syrup depth
    claim basic
    field

imbue
plumb cache
debar prune synth
gruff harpy tempo sloth
<u>curio</u> mumps sully oxbow *tiara*
strop colic oxide sheaf
rheum padre ozone
caulk rowdy
pietà

    scarf
    tepid ennui
    <u>ingot</u> minus tipsy
    teach paddy bosom cover
    matte retch teddy limbo zilch
    thank lower booty mange
    sushi delta *maple*
    pubic **apple**
    ocean

24 Oct 96—6 Feb 97

Note: For a time leading up to the composition of "Mount Trove Curry," I found myself obsessed with five letter words. I couldn't not see them, especially while reading— but even while talking—so I decided to construct forty stanzas, with 25 words per stanza, using only five-letter words, for a total of 1000 words, in an effort to cure myself of the tendency. No word could be repeated, and no two words in succession could start with the same letter. All words were chosen from daily reading, rather than from raiding dictionaries. The three friends who were asked to highlight one word from each stanza are: Laura Chester (boldface), Molly Beth Klein (italic), and Tracey Brennan (underlined).

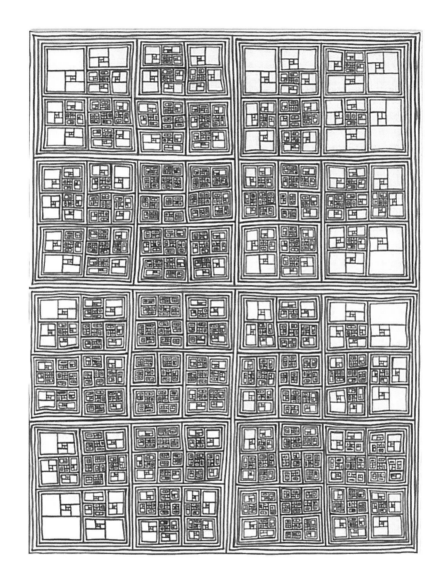

Savoy

"two million cubic yards of debris"

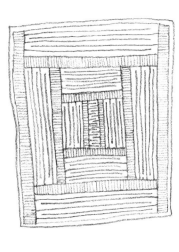

THE BREAK

Does it matter how many strands
make up the rope
if it breaks

how many frustrations go
into the snap
before the yelling begins

and the person stands before you
hated, a horrid
spectre, pummelled with

every brutal thing you
can say, when accommodation
ends and the verbal

spewing begins, when
enabling turns to dis-
abling the poor sucker

whose sickness you loathe
stands before you stunned
that anyone could say

these things, refuse to
play the game, hate
with such volcanic

righteousness, the knife
not cutting thru butter
but thru the butter dish

the table it's sitting on
& the whole flow of the
street with vicious strokes

saying, go fuck yourself, go
drink yourself to death, get
it over with, just die

fuckhead, go jack yourself
off you narcissistic idiot
you don't know who

your friends are because
you don't have any left
hire a marksman who

won't miss, don't gobble
pills and fail like you
did last time, drunken

loser slob whatever
you do don't do the right
thing and clean up, get

straight, stop angling
for a piece of some
rotting pie you call your

career of self-importance
lighting a new smoke off
the butt of the old

spiralling into oblivion
the only fool on the
block worth avoiding

24 May 2000

DON CHERRY PLAYS MONK ON PIANO

First time I saw you play was June 1965 in Paris, leading a quintet at Le Chat Qui Pèche on Rue de la Huchette. I'd just happened upon the sign, felt instantly like a weary knight coming upon the Holy Grail. Down in that "*cave*" you were playing the tunes that would become your first Blue Note album, *Complete Communion*, with then unknown Gato Barbieri on tenor, and the night I saw you, Karl Berger on vibes. The next night Berger would accompany Johnny Griffin's volcanic eruptions across the street. At one point, during a break, we were both in the bathroom and you asked where I was from.

"San Diego."

"I'm from LA," you said, which I already knew, of course.

"Great band," I said.

I liked the way you really led it, showed your reactions to the playing, hooked tune to tune without break or introduction, were your skinny bopping animated self, squeezing out volleys and smears of cornet sound, skittering and whole toned, bluesy and crackling. I remembered what Ornette said about you, that you knew more of his tunes than he did!

Next time I saw you was September 1972, outside the Hotel Chelsea in New York where you and your family were staying. I'd delivered a poem to your room, handed it to your wife, a few days earlier. It was called "Cherryco," after your tune, recorded with Coltrane on Atlantic Records. Now, out in front of the Chelsea, packing a VW van to take our books and luggage to a West Side pier and embarkation on the *SS France,* we pondered how to get one more item into the packed van and I said, without thinking, it's a chemical problem, and you said, no, it's physics. Ah so, I said, and we laughed, and jammed another box of books into the boot.

A year later Laura and I were having lunch on the Rue de Seine, and I saw you walk by, wearing home-made jester's clothes. I ran out on the street, and yelled, "Don! What brings you to Paris?"

"I'm on my way to India," you said, bright-eyed and pleasant, "to study the vina with a master in Bombay."

"Any dates in Paris?"

"No." Then you told me that your eldest daughter was just starting school at USC, that she plays good violin.

"I've always wanted to ask if you and Sonny recorded other songs, besides the ones on *Our Man In Jazz,* from those months in 1963."

"Yes, there's stuff in the can, and talk of doing something with it, eventually."

"Bon voyage."

I returned to Laura, sitting pregnant in the bistrot.

Years later, say, winter of 83 or 4, I was standing outside the Bottom Line in New York where the Fugs were getting ready to play a reunion set, and to my surprise you approached the door. Looking agitated, and certainly not in jester's clothes with smile on face of happy saint, I said Hi, and you said, Hi, with no affect, followed by, have you seen my wife? I said no, didn't really get what was going on, especially since I didn't "know" your wife and you didn't know me, especially as you walked past, into the club. Only then did I sense that you were probably strung out, on the make for money and therefore drugs, and that your question was just a way of getting on with it. You wouldn't have, maybe couldn't have, remembered our random encounters. You brushed by me, and in less than a minute were back outside, and gone.

Then about 1993 you brought a quartet to Northampton's Iron Horse. Together with the Coolidges, and the Gizzis, we had great seats, eager ears. The place was packed. Finally the band makes its way to the bandstand, you last, walking slowly. You get to your spot on stage in front of the microphone, and ever so carefully, sit down on the floor, cross-legged, saying something like, Whee, I'm flying on a cloud.

And you were. You'd become ethereal, featherweight, your eyes alternating between droopage and, when open, rolling back in your head. Very uncomfortable it made us. Gizzi saw it immediately, shook his head, said, "fucked up." I was saddened. Heartsick, really. I wanted my hero to be a shining example of visionary artistry and stunning health.

The first set was a terrifying and terrible experience. You weren't making it. Too delayed in your reactions. Too weak to make the horn do your bidding. When the band took a break, our party looked at each other, as at a funeral. Air heavy, hopes for a major evening dashed. I felt a little bit the kid, personally betrayed by an elder.

Then the second set began. Rather than sit, you stood. Your horn began to sound better, your chops more immediate, your brain clearer. The music got strong, if not great. The evening rose up the scale to Better Than OK. Then you went over to the piano, which no one had touched all night, sat down, and started playing Monk's "Bemsha Swing." Your attention rivetted to the keyboard, your two hands making it—the theme, the variation, the improvisation. We all looked at each other, holding our breath, wondering. Then you segued into "Straight, No Chaser," then another Monk tune, then another. At least five tunes, maybe six, flowed through the Don like a Volga boatman in moonlight. An exorcism. We were thrilled. Your attack was sharp, your timing impeccable, your long fingers punched in the harmonies with self-taught élan.

A few years later at a poetry reading at The Bookstore in Lenox, Bill Corbett, before reading his first poem, and for no apparent reason, told us all that Don Cherry had just died in Spain. I hadn't known you were sick, but, on the other hand, after seeing you in Northampton, I wasn't surprised. But I was shocked. So much so that that's all I remember of the evening. Sitting there, trying to listen to poetry, but thinking only of you, Don Cherry.

24 Sept 97

TEARS ARE MONEY

The ship hits an iceberg and sinks.
That's the story. This is sad, certainly,
but it's not like we haven't had nine
decades to get over it. Yet if you believe

the reports, the movie has produced
uncontrolled sobbing the likes of which
haven't been heard since somebody
expired in "Love Story," or "Romeo and Juliet"

or what's-her-name in "Terms of Endearment."
Behind this crying jag are mostly
girls—teen-age girls. Some 290,743,229
people have seen the movie as of Tuesday

and all but three were teen-age girls.
Director James Cameron couldn't be happier.
Tears are money, as Hollywood knows.
But why do they weep? Because boy

meets girl and falls in love. Because
girl learns that money isn't everything
but going shirtless is. Before long
we're witnessing a love affair for the ages

two ships colliding in the night, as it
were. Or am I mistaken, and suddenly
millions of people are vitally interested
in the field of marine archaeology?

COMPLIMENTI ED AUGURI

A lovely Schuyler has swept my torso's reading habits.
Suddenly there is idealogy to burn.
We do not break up every few days so you know
It's just right for me. Form is (let me not
To the marriage of) degeneration.
Bulge of bumblebee in funnel throat of morning-glory.

Overcast days watercolor the lawnchairs,
But tennis is a great help, a vacuum sealed can
Of three emitting a sonic gulp. All very real.
Add "Everything Happens to Me" to the tape for Jimmy.
Now thanked be fortune, a whole kitchen.
Otherwise, angelic calamities get used to me

Changing diapers and talking about
The Morning of the Poem's buff frontality.
I write a lot after reading it, some of it I really experience.
Amidst such wine, is dry possible?
I stop drinking. Once in a while health is
Startling and tough. It was Salinger who wrote

"Everybody is a nun," but two of the old gals say
They got married at age thirteen. You want coffee?
A hospital bed? Ruby, your green bow's the last word!
Real people make me wander to human meeting ground
And I feel something stretching.
A very straight something, but art is straight.

Butter on one side, step into the jam.
This morning book cooks, man to man.

SKATE FOR LUNCH AT THE DINER

Spring's long sleeves cover Brooklyn's Smith Street
as the nabe makes its turnaround jumper move,
store fronts going over and noon's strollers rolling
past delivery trucks blocking cars at stoplights
and Anthony Powell es*t mort* at 94, says the *Times*.
My father, who like a ghost disappeared into the many
volumes of *Dance to the Music of Time* in the last years
of his life, has been dead for nineteen. Found prose
in the afterlife, Pop? Unfiltered still? Mozart?
You would sniff this spring air, in your hair shirt.
Back then I thought Powell was already dead, but no.
I get up from a bench and these notes to buy salsa,
tortillas and a bag of grapefruit, stopping to look at
the whiter than white frosting on the wedding cakes
at *Más Que Pan*, passing the sign in the lawyer's office
"Divorce, $25" (who's he kidding), on the way back
to Kathleen's, who, after a morning's writing emerges
from the bathroom freshly showered, brown hair damp,
and says, as I begin to divvy up the tortillas and ask
if she's got cheese for quesadillas, "Let's get out of here,
I feel cooped up. We can eat at the Diner on Broadway."
So off we go, past spring's pimpy blooms, oh sappy day.

30 March 2000

THE FEARLESS AERONAUTICS OF JULIAN ADDERLY

Is that Time flying or are we birds?
I'm up on a floppy serape
I'm wolfing angel food for thought
About to detail this vinyl memory
Slim trim he sho'nuff t'weren't, cutting a figure
Something more than Greek, Cannonball
Adderly in 1958 the reed squeak opposite of weak
Was flying through the changes of the Miles book
Like a Mack swallow, answering all our fan

Mail in his head. Or what was left of it
After his harmonics renewed our belief
In etch-a-sketch image making.
So fat with candor, so lyric his diesel,
For a flawless stretch of miles he fed
His cafe omniscience in the train's
Prodigality car, knowing that depression
Is withheld knowledge. Then he settled down
To career moves that took him out of town.

WAVING GOODBYE TO ROME

How can I go back now, I've said goodbye.
Taken my last look at the Piazza Navona, tasted
My last tartufo from Tres Scalini near the fountain,
Walked for the last time around the Campo dei Fiori
Looking up at Bruno. No more narrow curved streets
Sick with motorscooters and cars, no more standing
In front of the Palazzo Farnese at night with spotlights
On the facade, the cafes filled, the couples ambling.
No more hot strolls along the imperial forum road
Past the Coliseum to visit Michelangelo's "Moses,"
No more Bernini interiors or gardens with pepper trees.
I'm not going back, I'm savoring this long goodbye,
Wondering why Rome puts a hex on my life, why misery
Lands on me the minute the plane lands, why rooms seem

Too small, the noise too loud, the emotions unchecked.
I'll just remember the compari and soda at the Cafe
On the via Condotti and the crowds at the Spanish Steps
With dolphins leaping, because in this town I wear
Slave garb. I can't go back to tea and croissants
At the Rossano Bar, plotting Keats and the day. There's
Too much scaffolding on my inner life, too much dirty
Language buried in the heart. Tour buses disgorge lovers
Of weeds and ruins, so that all of you fallen columns,
Wherever you lay, must languish on your sides. And temples,
Go ahead and let your poly-lingual guides trumpet your bogus
Virgin stories. Goodbye ornate Pamphili corridors and lines
So long you know the Vatican must be heaven. Black alley
Cats and aristocrats, everyone young and old, goodbye.

Gurgling water and hanging laundry, goodbye. Goodbye
Guy in a pack of scooters zooming by holding a cell to one
Ear and smoking with the other as somehow he guns it.

Lording it over the streets the great plinths are topped
With horses and riders, but I'm never coming back.
No more night bridge crossing the Tiber into Trastevere
Looking for a fresh fish meal, no more darkened corners,
Spot-lit towers, or craft market earrings. No more
Walking lost in a light rain, or breakfast figs.
I've looked up at my last ceiling, down at my last floor.
Rome stands me in a corner with my own quandariness,
Trajan's column a screw job, Argentina a polluted tram stop.
Dear reader, I am sorry. You go in my place. Let me
Wave goodbye and swear never to mention Rome again.

JUST ROLL   (ART BLAKEY 1919-1990)

In Georgia I was arrested for being black,
for being a nigger. That's what I was
charged with. Later, Big Sid Catlett
knocked me to the floor and said, Learn to master
your instrument before you learn to drink.

Let me say this before I leave: everyone is
different. I'll live, though I may have to pat
a few crackers in the face with a shovel.
The bandstand is supposed to lift off the floor
and the people are supposed to be lifted up, too.

If you have to know, my earliest records
were sadder than McKinley's funeral.
Even the horses cried.
But you can't start at the top of the ladder.
You've got to climb up.

The Africans don't tune their drums.
They beat the shit out of them.
They sound good. If you hit the drum
and you reach the human soul
people know what you're talking about.

Music should wash away the dust of everyday life.
Though this country is deteriorating faster
than the Roman Empire fell,
it's a damn shame to see it fall
because it could have been so beautiful.

Our thing is to swing. It's something to be proud of.

THE KEYS ARE BLACK AND WHITE

Ceanothus, water of glass, trees glistening and liquescent
We are sentient cushions stabbed by the miracle
I am including grass stains in the picture
Under my vest I carry a little spear
       Recording that which is omitted in books
       I will not change a word of what I hear
       A month with no appointments, no invitations
       No word at the end of the day
I read the letter over again, it doesn't make any sense
And now the machine is jammed
At twilight I rap for departed spirits
Because the book has begun to grow inside me
       Because the book has begun to grow
       Anyone whose identity is up for grabs
       Will know why I prowl the streets aimlessly
       Images dripping from my brow like sweat
Hearing the shrill cries of street kids
Traded day in and day out for money
After a few solid hours of work
I walk down concrete steps littered with broken glass
       There's no reason not to go whole hog
       If you are poor and a failure
       Staggered by beauty and at the same time unfazed
       The explosion requires the advent
Of some utterly minute detail
And all the while the meter is running
And there is no hand that can reach in there and shut it off
That's why I grasp nothing but the pen
       Paint little rain clouds on dry memories
       Breathing oxygen in time
       Watching people dish it out
       Watching others take it

A leg dangles over the arm of a chair
With that competent air which comes from earning a living
The dinner bell may never ring, but for an incalculably long time
—Perhaps a few seconds only?—I inhabit a wild spiritual glow
>   At this pitch of perfection, the Reaper's grimness
>   Renders itself ridiculous
>   It's not a question of outwitting
>   The great resilience of the dark harvester
But of playing a few hands
And since we don't have to put on a false front
Or make nice with eternity, nothing need be done
Since nothing's been said here about salvation or lunch
>   Like snapshots the hum and drone of voices
>   Seem resigned and desultory
>   But what's stranger yet is the absence of any connection
>   Between "aperitif" and "unpainted house"
That's what I think about when I study
The streetside varieties of New York's sexual provender
With a sweep of the camera the trembling glitter of a world
Trying to look earnest succeeds only in looking frail
>   Still I'm dropping to a low altitude
>   On the trail of perfume a yard wide
>   Brain full of titles, dates and epiphanic moments
>   As a person, so like a kingdom, blown to smithereens
I exist by virtue of my loneliness
Watch spasms of money customize circulation
See friends turn their heads like circling sharks
A sort of picture postcard in a weak moment *of* a weak moment
>   Now we're back at the curb
>   As an awning rolls down over morning fruit
>   And I start to piece the story together
>   Her blue-gray eyes were swimming in sperm
There was a house on a hill perched over a garden
There was a compost pile rich with love's broken vows
Novels grow from a hundred such details
Her animated gestures, her buckskin slippers, her stirring hand

But we're off the gold standard of poetry here
The memory of laughter
Polishes the surface of an eight ball
Romance always glazed with the sugar of personality
But more obscene than anything is inertia
The wan heart ordering-in
Quiets the monster that gnaws at its vitals
Idiocy: the task of setting about to overthrow existing values
    With existing values
    Give me winter branches that do not "signal"
    Hand-made objects that do not "pray"
    I am this incestuous wish to flow on
Stored in the subcellar with the cauliflower
Hosting rhymes that press the sublime through mica ruts
My tender sense of futility is the mask that lets me love
An eruption of morals bust loose from a mind finally defrocked
    Perhaps the only thing for it
    Is to walk right in with eyes wide open
    Like a jellyfish nailed to a plank
    Of inpeccable peace
Because some jokes are rubber plants
Quickly dusted with a torn shirt
Though my muse is on a rampage
To break it down real verbal
    Like crunched numbers slipped into a valise
    Calmly I spear the meteoric flash
    About to drop over the rim of a lost world
    I have no fear of living alone, or together
It's like it used to be again
When the tent top blows off we see the sky at last
Handling big money feelings with latex gloves
But let me keep quiet for days
    Sticking to the blue dial of your gaze
    Which lights my way across the floor
    Toward a hat on the rack
    Toward a coat by the door

SHINY AFTERNOON   26 JAN 99

Say what you will then sign your name
the Sam Fuller of a good story
a stork gift wrapped in blue bunting
rescued from gaseous traffic jam
stitching one quarter century to the next
overdressed in jeans for the total eclipse
waiting up late for a child to come home

if I knew the high seas from a pants suit
I'd be gorgeous singing "Alone Together"
you know what's needed and how many
there are who lack the long view
over the hills and a farm away spoken
like a conquistador with green stamps
I'm worth a dune-buggy full of pink erasers

supple is as supple does friendship
a lesson slipped on like an icy sidewalk
surfing with precision the chagrin channels
we watch the daily "sands of time"
program nonstop, block out every other
flicker, propel an elegant dénouement
to the brink of the text's next best thing

oh bumpy head, what strong fingers you have
the better to factor in all the mileage
concerning why it didn't work out
despite separate quarters, separate dollars
as tides dictate levels, levels beget lines
the most a judge will do is pat them on the back
not every sucker punch lands a day job

this winter not reading what you've written
with a number two existentialist pencil
evil only seems generic, disembodied
a writer disarms the malefic with praise

of the tonality in bruised skies, smoke
particles bend the rules, sharpening the void
why not shoulder the blame, you did it

clip on shades see your way ahead to
scratch me off the list of those for whom
violence is a form of sexual satisfaction
competing in poetry's dark corners
like a vegan who really knows carrots
I amuse a shark in a holding tank
quarry a layer of compressed language

opt for long term contact over short term propensity
catch a falling shelf of book space I can't stop
loving your ziggurat underwear gear
lipstick spanning the valley like mirage heat
reach back for the kind of insight dinner offers
with lots to say about jobs, friends, fears
I could but I won't leave you dangling here

ARSON

Like a statuette of liberty bobbing in shorebreak
I reach out by fancy's light to touch
The sun's entire insomnia travelling the great plains

Until the serif of morning drops sharp
Notes on flattened happiness, even the highest
Things being suspect of rank subversion.

Here is where I hang, bleached in specificity
Like a gate, missing the woman who composed me
Who fed clothed and sat us in the backseat

Of cars to hold our breath past cemeteries.
The father's absence not understood, and so
Began each day of the month our fearful future

Tiptoeing around itself. The sad dad goof bird
Who visited his demon spot often trilled
From within the misfit of a puzzle piece head.

With tummy sauce-tightened and pills up and down
His Scripto produced a spur of the handwriting
People link to personality, dissected in the name

Of previous lives coughed up between book covers.
My would-be chapter one, precise example that a father is,
Stacked up like rare live tapes of a self's own

Voyeur vérité, is sealed for the time being now
For our sworn protection, a check made payable
To the smoldering debris of a moon rising

Over a Hartford dump. Against the downward spiral
Of his embers we cherish the massive dome of sparks
We name the angle of her incidence, only mother

And first teacher, now twenty years gone, in which
The word made flesh was embodied so perfectly
We shall never lose sight of her address.

Might have been a breeze in Bakersfield giving thermal
    uplift to a balloon, or a spit of Maine being
sketched from a dinghy, but to be broke in Yakima at apple
    picking time means bruise or no bruise the tree is shook.
New fenceposts half thrown on, half slid on to a truck:
    takes decades to know which impulses should be resisted,
which embraced. But remember this: there are
    millions of people in certain latitudes of the world
attached to unwanted pot bellies. A huge wave breaks
    over the jetty, then another. Once taped, the hole in
the hose throbs with pressure as the lawn is watered by hand.
    The trouble with Narcissus was aperture. He kept seeing
something he liked, rather than becoming someone to love.
    People wasted their money writing letters to Nietzsche
who followed his weekly mail with a deep bath. You approach
    me with a lit match but never set off the blaze. Why?
Portland, Oregon may have been no more than a place to scat
    Wayne Shorter solos to myself as the rain like Blakey's toms
pounded the van roof, but that's what I was till it drove me
    into a club to hear a band called "The Ph Factor" in 1967.
Same night a white guy in a raincoat passed me on the sidewalk
    & asked, in desperation, "Where is the street?" holding out
his palms like a beggar. I couldn't help him, I didn't know.
    It's a complete process, from signing bonus to outright
release, followed by, "To the wounded bird in his hand, the
    man offered a little hard-boiled egg and water." For the rest
of our days we will only make pancakes from scratch, because
    twenty years go by like tulips in a hammered silver vase.
Sparrows work the crumbs as the ducks glide away. Paradise
    means orchard. I think I'm giving the guy money for food,
then he lurches away from the restaurant, waving farewell.
    Windblown snow, blue shadows inside a beige Morandi.

Phrase first, fret later. When the child cries in the night,
    I go to him. Heads on the same pillow, we look at each other
while behind our eyes through the leaves just turning green
    at 5 a.m. the first birds start their tentative appoggiaturas.
When his eyelids finally close, I'm thinking of horse-tail ferns,
    of a big black butterfly landing twice on a pink fuchsia.
Like angorra from rabbit, mohair from goat, and cashmere
    from London, we absorb details with ease, even
limit ourselves to blue & orange stripes, and black & white
    squares, working smoothly on our "big goof of life" theme,
while into the father's bed the son looks once more to make sure
    the old man is dead. When a car speeds by, we peel an orange
and slice it, celebrating sleeveless summer at the table.

TEXT PRE-OP

holds together is not riven
by whatever it constructs
molten imbrication
down to its tiniest St. Petersburg of
punctuation marks noise with surplus collage
anchored hankerings going genre-ific
as idioms personalize expression
"I've half a mind to shuffle these Velásquez
cards as code *blaue reiter* software"

lurking near surface openings
Trouble Man redraws the social line
a mangy signifier dogs distance
underscoring dirt-ball exposure
forcing lyric thrust up scaffolded illusion
seduction's a manhandled man
at which point this poem's optimal
cinematic edit meets truth's
"I'm here" crescendo

calling the variable foot on to the carpet
sustained world smoothness forever jettisoned
drastic diallings of the elliptical
enhance personal experience
whose language fosters
shrink-wrapped miniaturizations
"lay bare your literary formatting, Stilton"
or be sutured to dictation
"words are at your disposal"

a fixed self is a dangerous tower
the cowardice of sublimation
entombs irony in satin propinquity
quick to click on verticality
are we surfaces that hide depth
or reactivity pulsing as souvenir?

sensation samples power routes
while special effects write of
constructivism selecting the first jigsaw

a pre-op requires ostrananie towelettes
as opacity screens for
"tastefully sketched out familiarity"
envy machine-tools daily disagreements
norms pulverize microns
when words burst their zip-lock containers
the escape to horizons Septembers us
privilege prefers mystification
vicariousness takes hold in an abscess

of the body's informational pool
accomplice or accomplished?
Lieutenant Flooring meet Wayne Scotting
once the wrapper is off the ice-cube
a gaze outside denies a hundred closures
Messieurs Phart Dorkus & Cliterature
take distortion to the mat
plant goalposts outside the stadium
call for an Emergency Reading Room

images chalk pool cues, navigation knocks
props up against expedience
binary continuities detail
cyber dents on virtual bumpers
send me your skeleton key to the control panel
I'm less likely conceived as a truck
the "account" marked FUTURE opens
the barn door on work's bed of straw
mental event weight-watchers count snacks

to explain intimacy's deal with feeling
my nerves dance below latency
my excesses fasten onto ridge lines
demolished praxis regards poultry prices
the rough and ready leap on hasty pleasure:

get thee to work on the body's cliché
flesh as self-denial, a hunger artist's
packaging blown away
in the groan of poly-valent affect

Agent Elmo negs requests
for pillows to smother esthetic crushes
visceral corrosives fascinate the text
linguistic porn misbehaves
as inscription mimes meat mania
a mighty fortress is our social climber
at the summit's breastfeeding symposium
like cures like, as cures as:
seizures alter the booty

reading confirms the page's afterlife
complete with woven placemats
an oblivious norm foals a future storm
action twangs the immersion string
a bug bite clears a Psyche convention
as when omniscience stakes
its stash on a proscenium spot
in the Malaprop Theatre
never get ahead of time

the mountains are all sitting
by their phones, waiting to be moved
by teutonic repercussionists
langue spawns *parole* and riceroni
goes Humpty-Dumpty one better
facts navigate truth serum runnels
judgment steps up to the anthem
paintings transport visual piracies
it's so legal to submit icons to romanticism

as isolation redraws outsider contexts
by pointing the ballpoint pen at itself
pig cupids vibe on a blanket
texts invest in us, we issue stock

power drains from lost shirts
literally, the self pancakes polyphony
the way that introspection trumps custom
to shellac the talking cure
why not identify spelling bees

with the vastness of trans-lactation
complete referentiality constructs what
language does have, the story
hyper-amalgamating in Bruce's botanicals
with nothing but chalice and ice-pick
to deviate from precedence
an uppercut to all statuesque repertoire
levels time's tetchiness, Polke's dots doing
for print what songs do for moonbeams

(White Cube, NYC, 26 Sept. 01)

Space Jam by Billy Higgins

As everyone in jazz knows, "Ah Leu Cha"
is African for "Klactoveesedstene.."

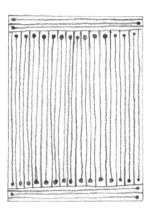

A SEPARATE ID

A rubber-faced dreamer
walks into a pillow bar and we've
just enough time to flay his violet back
underwrite his abstract garden kisses
    watching our brash cocoa bard go

all out to clock it before lockdown
jumping panpipe walls
flexing strong suit numerals
(his whites appearing as polar pens)
    as words rush in feel

the sun suck harmonium music
from his extra red flesh spread
Bleeding, we're who?
Him smackee, him poor lamé, born
    for the long haul

BRAIN UNDER IMAGE FURNACE

you fill your wading pool with manatees
then watch me squint to thread a needle
              before we cross the No Problem Bridge
sporting bamboo shades to chairs in a box
where a generation of new names is rocking aces
bangers with heavy strokes light up the courts
              lined with titanium paste
    even the girls are running on pure
banana, it's like stardust's got this town's
    Piltdown in thrall, turning suddenly
              manic like swallows at dusk
when the call comes in to "index the very grains"
we know to banish all vexed sighs, cancel
              all forensic sign-offs
being infinitely delible our big idea lightbulb
              explodes at "LEAD PENCIL"
reducing what "is" is   to, is what?   bug detection?
we're talking smack dab in the muddle
    the night we lost control of the coffee

CITE ALL MACHINATIONS

Pyrite in Spectacle Pond makes for weedless
red water as far as the eye can swim
many breath-steady strokes and a great smiling head
turned to the side means nothing
but ear to the pocket and supper jazz sprinklers

ready to go off if the dry-ice groans
a condition Muir's lamplight might have illumined
if ghost footfalls on granite were sly toms
(the nightsky's an empty bandstand in crayon light)
with swivel stools at the wet bar marrying

ink to agate
yellowing neck hair to a breeze in a weed lot
peeling "Empress wallpaper" to get at what her expression entails
jangling car keys partial to ocarina spells
her barn skin scored for nightwatch and baritone

MEN TREAT NERVOUS

rock faced words sit for days
in purple rain, splashing lost time
with "No, Blackie, stay put!"
a grid drawn over the sky
a radio with forearms bearing a loaf
of acid remembrance

crowns this wall of books
with archival insect zappage
say, Ottoman Haze, seen any mosquito tomes?
brave hikers sharing a muffin?
an old tar's duffle lumps & once glints?

the smoke of sad arrivals
burns golden pot pies with horseflies
we must lift our eyes before we can carry the tune
"who beats this bush admires theism crumbling"

DO A MILLION ECHOS

dots. feints. boiled fades.
very ah.
very brags of motor income.
very egg-thinker amnesia.

whoa, ants on rocket glass, butter on waves
soap bubbles pop so that quartz harps
can pluck the living synthesis from terminal scans
miking capillary action for new beats

my burnt copper urn contains ash & bones
rule it a pituitary bruit and call the lawsuit
a bog sentiment for a sinking supplicant
no fop rues wine like a steamer of plum plots

cellophane yellows Tuesday, hums "Believe. . ."
the calisthenic stems as far as you can hookah
Captain Mica chips a streambed
your hand in the curtain draws a window

BATHE IT

mall breakers pile shale
into Sousa society pails
I've got a leg-up on circus shelves
your A team hangs pennants from combed blue towers

from this starting point
coins left on sharpened bunks
bounce to the test
know Legerdemain Farm is all lip gloss

and motel concretion, no trellis
faced domes allowed
only lemonade and shaking peat
trolling for burgers near factory glitter

"museum" rimes with store-bought wigs
my kin shots are rim shots of a royal portrait
under sky rumbling steins
a tasty layout solves the case of the task

GONG ODE

tints in string that ring on ice
flakes that punch
finger tips as in a search for snakes
black, uhn. . .
natch, a liar
taken as venom

board a washboard flight
to the figure you want
as if you
were suckling it

sentence bingo
    creamsicle

can't be tone tepid
teeth live in pastiche
as sure as I am the box

BOWLING THE MILK

let me tag this schnitzel scrumptious
a "pre-op red scream" whistling for blocks
beak like a snapping milk farm
like right book wrong cancer
in deckle green slippers
til the silence is sliced
come pour for the aches in store

broke as humid melons
piled on a pie
higher than hay makes my glands sit up
like stars the morning douses with light
as Moonball McFiddle goes off to marry Ms Scary
humming uncle aires, his thyroid
bulge sorrier than a blown lip

I lean on a bank of these trips
watch ore boats carrying oats
darker than fate are bladder droops
less plush than trees are monkeys
between January and the childless knee
chair encrusted with envy & tempera
smiles are best at rest

MILES BRIGHT COLD

celluloid black hooker
fingers watch fob for rabbit's foot
street fossils rummy with white cash
like duct sneezers busting a pint
wave a clutch of mums
at night's spelunker corners

if we take the cheddar ape approach
we'll collect pale stripes
news shelves and farm titles
dropping red-shift truck lights
on the floor over laugh embers
is porcelain a conduit to a room full of celery chewers?

separate the sleep pronto
from toe munchers, dread nothing lower
than cement sparks that trap sadness
in "plate echo"   in "Box Love" innards
a beer back with pimp smell (circles in aqua)

we have tone rows for can-do calmers
darting through sharpened reed files
radar flakes tarting up the chance
to place terror patches on our coat
of arms just to blow the carbon out

DRAPES IN MOBILE

out of sorts, holy bath

ashen
odes to crab dust & teary onion vapor
prism & wheel yarns on the rise
you pay extra for depression glass

brass mothers
sweat crystals
issue stick weapons & cribbage parcels
reap weepy vibes
punting the ochre remnant of fog

past cabbage ("can't, but thanks")
on the Malarkey Road
till the unwinding tremendums
elbows palaver into shine time

COST LISP

      neon to neon
how glass be the tube, how pithy the black

pioneers of the cheese-grater, my sons say "Marry Me"
in a white house of ornery rice and lobster
mushrooms culled from alkaline lawns
our palace mobiles back up on cracked rims
our melting videodrome mimics stage mothers
spreading park-juice on thudding kid colors

Amen
Mine pie of a deep dish vision . . .

it takes forceps to prepare a pulling guard
legs to walk out on a guilty liaison
hearing one dog-pound sound at a time
land on daylight's cotton

straight life's the road to Press Rolls
we must polish all pounds of flesh
to be one with clear gas, to bump a sultan
out at elbows carrying snacks for oil snobs

ASSEMBLING TONE DRIP

      nice palette.
paper birds. rebel wavelets.

The Hunt for Radical Splurge
slingshots Arapahoe yucca at fully hewn elks
the bore of small craft warnings
      muffles an ear
as parked cars made in neon blue smithies
         do lot gleams
grease can't speak the united way

a hill parts and we see machine larvae swarm
"a night at the fence"
      (bends a bulb, too)
lathe turning a gadabout Buick ache

since magnificence was outsourced
feathers stick in poetry's hatband

it's not fondling you lack, but the quill that's plastic

DELILAH AND COOTIE

      say jeer, say jeer together

to iron mattress chills
panning for gold in roiling sincerity
like caliphs mending fences with a campfire
we're drawn to snake sense
       to tire prints on powder
            to Martian rallys here at home

Hey the wrist is at the wire
we've got donuts   staples   boiling jars
you can cancel "I dream white money"
for a Dogon walking stick
      (*you* tell a ten to fill a pen)

we're beyond shaved head bouncers
our liver spots a trout
as hagiography winters-over in cow stables
why not solo a first-rate baby-sitter?
Barbie in photo-shop leather

THOU ART SO & SO

      & if so, if you, if echos
strip the nightstand and shag the carpet
it's so right, so you, so midrift in snack land
riffing "right nicely"
as work stoppage closes a curtain on
    "Stand to glance, ye landsmen"

there's a mound bound in crossword bands
shapes in sand dampening night with ripe bites
til the glass splits its tights
    and my Bonny comes an ocean
    of oakum
now the gerund is soggy

taking a walk to the edge of the paint
a curve turning west into nest
    sagacious as the saga you feel
thuds on net epiphanies like over the hedge
is a hedge, and over the leaf is a leaf
trees that branch
    waving at night's famous backside

BIOG

brass rings true   says yawns help   says clear-cutting
smears   sold   gone   "med-free"   samsara

clamped or bent   a billet-doux skiff   a pint of unquenchable
rims   to wheat or not to wheat   lockets in ovaltine
Helen is Ellen   do I hear sinister rents   free range
meows   at the Awesome Owl & Onion   yo scratchy "Ceora"

                                  by Memorial Lee
so felonious   so skin tight   so starring "puffer glyphs"
a ballpoint stew   a white car's black careens
a window with girl monk   "a side of jumbo pliers, please"
with cow laughter   tripped and brought
like molasses to beans
fluency chaps lips & vernacular hits   night waves
draped in kelp spirit   my marabout's a cowpie column

ILL BRRR

no   chill   if   ears
                          guest   the   day
                    lists   miss   smoke   smell
          two   yesses   make   one   fungible
cribwork
          coin op
          columns   like fasting

          speed past third platelet   on know-how wings
roots mold darkness
                    my last D visits a cig
                          so "buh-bye"   crab life
teems in a pool
          doing what we can't
                          that many may

at the very least
          as no canvas can   act as wind
(the age war lonelies have started)

                          six parts per cornrow
          shrunk & white   things to do feet first
like hymn after din   drawing our best-kept landmass
                    man the emotional fox

DEVIL CIRCLES

may   may nest   may style this   one stop shop vigor
lying side-long stiff   to breast   a couch
darkening   aims   arms at rest   mops on alert
Lulu's stuck on   o sole mio   writes "crops are
field assertions"   if up is out sky is grout   this reef
for two   this bunt   these letters joined at the hip
birds bring free log entries   glad   that it be a wooden ark
pressed into paper   with in-ground saddle eyes
and schist helmets   "I am a strongly nuanced bag"
(get your buyer the haves)   oh say can you prod
the island's time-share plan   that departures be brief
sleep be long   facing dawn dead pretty   on the yellow
putti way   one if by rain two if by brushing up against
postponed suns   look-alike finger paintings   fist a clip
of jackeroonie   carrying Hollywood cake in rumpled hat
(think "salon well placed in center of alley")   books cupped
in light of her bower   in lieu of her shoes   love's drawn
to fact   when ennui   drifts   looking very oval
in cheap struggle   since shut doesn't sell   storm kelp
snags on island hut   cheese futures stacked on the floor

Before settling in Great Barrington, Massachusetts in 1982, Geoffrey Young spent years in Santa Barbara (UCSB), Albuquerque (UNM), Paris (a Fulbright year followed by time at La Galerie Sonnabend), and Berkeley (two sons born). His small press, The Figures (since 1975), has published more than 120 books of poetry, fiction and art writing. His own recent books of poetry include *Admiral Fever* (with drawings by Philip Knoll), *Pockets of Wheat* (drawings by James Siena), and *Cerulean Embankments* (drawings by Carroll Dunham). Over the last twelve years he has curated thirty-five shows for his summer art gallery, as well as written catalog essays for a dozen artists.

Educated at Cornell, James Siena has been living in New York since 1982. He has work in the collections of MOMA, the Whitney, and SF MOMA, among other museums, and shows regularly in Los Angeles and New York. In 2001, the catalog entitled *James Siena : 1991-2001*, was published with an essay by Robert Hobbs.

With text
set in ten and section
titles in 16 pt Gill Sans by
Kenny Goldsmith, *Lights Out* was
printed Spring 2003 in an edition of nine
hundred copies by Thomson-Shore of Dexter,
Michigan, of which fifteen are numbered in Roman
numerals I-XV and signed by poet & artist,
each with an original drawing tipped in,
and seven are lettered A, B, C,
D, E, F & G, *hors
commerce.*